Thanks—
THANKS A LOT

BABYLON BOOKS

THANKS— THANKS A LOT

★

BILLY PARKER
★ ★ ★ ★ ★ WITH ★ ★ ★ ★ ★
JOHN WOOLEY & BRETT BINGHAM

BABYLON BOOKS

Thanks—Thanks A Lot

© 2021 Billy Parker with John Wooley and Brett Bingham
All rights reserved. Published 2021.

No part of this book may be reproduced, stored in a retrieval system, or transmitted in any form by an electronic, mechanical, photocopying, recording means, or otherwise, without prior written permission from the authors.

ISBN-13: 978-1-954871-26-7

Babylon Books Publishing

Every effort has been made to trace the ownership of all copyrighted material included in this publication. Any errors that may have occured are inadvertent and will be corrected in subsequent editions, provided notification is sent to the publisher.

Cover and Interior Design by Müllerhaus Legacy.

Photo Acquisition by Brett Bingham and John Wooley unless otherwise noted.

DEDICATION

I would like to dedicate this book to my family...
Jerri, my wife of over 55 years now
My son Billy Joe, his wife Denise, and their children Billy and Sarah
My son Kris and his children Joshua, Gabriella, and Lauren
My daughter Liz, her daughter Amber, and Amber's son Asher
My daughter Kathy and her son Brandon
And our dog Molly

INTRODUCTION

To be honest with you, it took a little while for my good pals Brett and John to convince me that we should do a book about my life. As I've told 'em a lot more than once, I've never been a fan of *me*, and I honestly didn't think too many people would be interested in reading about stuff like how I grew up, how I got into the radio and country music business, and what I thought about the people I've worked with, the stars and the unknowns and all the folks in-between.

Brett and John didn't agree. They believed different—and I guess they still do.

Now that it's done, we're fixing to find out who's right.

We did the interviews for this book at my house, back in my den where I've got all the old mementos of my career in broadcasting and country music. The very first time we officially got together and Brett set his recorder down on the table next to me, John told me about writing a book with Ralph Terry, the great old New York Yankees pitcher from Chelsea, Oklahoma, and how they started it with the story of Ralph getting called up to the major leagues for the very first time, remembering how nervous and keyed-up he was until he threw that first pitch.

"Brett and I want to start the book with something like that from your career," he said. "So what we want you to do is think back to something that happened in your own life. Maybe it's what set you on the path to doing what you did in the music business. It could've been getting an award that let you know you were right in choosing to do what you did. It could've been standing in front of a big audience at some show, looking out over a cheering crowd."

He explained that something like that gives the folks reading the book—that's you—a little hook that gets them immediately into the story, and after we've got 'em interested with that anecdote we can go back and get into my childhood and all that stuff and they'll stay with us. That was the idea, anyway.

It seemed like a simple enough question, but I had to do a lot of thinking before I could answer—and I admit I changed my answer more than once. Because I've been really fortunate and blessed over my years in the country-music and radio business, I had a lot of high spots to choose from, career-wise. But I kept going back and forth in my own mind about which was the most important.

Would it have been the call I got from Cal Smith back in 1968, asking me if I wanted to go on the road with Ernest Tubb as the front man for his famous Texas Troubadours? Would it have been my first *Midnite Jamboree* radio show with Ernest, stepping up to the microphone live at midnight on the stage at his record shop in Nashville—or what happened just afterwards, when we all hopped into E.T.'s bus, the Green Hornet, and headed to Eau Claire, Wisconsin for a matinee show? It was a hell of a long way from Nashville, and I believe my knees knocked all the way there. I was a nervous wreck. But I got the job done, and for the next couple of years, I fronted E.T.'s band all over North America.

I also thought about the awards I was fortunate enough to get for being on the radio: four from the Academy of Country Music for Disc Jockey of the Year, and another one with the same designation from the Country Music Association. You can only win that last one once; I was fortunate enough to get it the year after the CMA first started giving it out.

With Brett and John jogging my memory, I thought back to what I felt like when I accepted those honors and looked over those big crowds in Nashville and L.A. as I stepped up to the mike to say thank-you's that did come right from my heart.

But then, I got to thinking about just *why* I'd been given those little statuettes. Looking at the row of awards over against the wall in my den, I knew they were there because of all the good listeners to my show, the ones who called in with requests or talked to me at my personal appearances or said hi to me on the street or in the grocery store or doctor's office, along with the many others I hadn't met and never would, those who picked up my show in other states, or local folks who just quietly enjoyed what they heard. I also wouldn't have gotten a single one of those awards without the artists I'd had the privilege of playing and, in many cases, having with me on the air, either in the studio or on the telephone. Many was the time that some performer, his or her tour bus pulled into some lonely truck stop at 3 a.m., called me from a pay phone to chat over the air on my all-night truckers' show for a few minutes before climbing back on board and heading back down that endless old highway

So it was the listeners and the artists that got me those awards. But it wasn't only them. Without radio station KVOO—the Voice of Oklahoma—and its 50,000 watts of pure radio power, I wouldn't have been anywhere. I sure wouldn't have been able to get my voice and my show heard throughout a whole lot of the USA and up into Canada. I was very fortunate to have begun my radio career in the old days before FM radio, when a big clear-channel AM signal like KVOO had could get a deejay and his music into homes and cars and trucks hundreds of miles away from his or her studio—in this case, all the way to California and nearly everywhere else except back East. Beginning nearly 40 years before I started there, KVOO's great range had helped Bob Wills spread the sound of western-swing music throughout America, thanks to the daily Wills broadcasts that got to most of the country.

At the same time I was doing my shows, I continued to be able to cut records and go out and do a little pickin' and grinnin.' And I know KVOO helped get my name out there to people who might not have heard of me otherwise. You may know—and you'll *sure* know it if you read this book—I'd been playing out and recording songs, including "Thanks A Lot," before KVOO, but I'd never had anything get into the national charts until after I started at the station. I'd had some stretches as a disc jockey, too, prior to joining KVOO, but it was there that the two parts of my career finally came together for good.

So, when it comes to the biggest moment in my life, I've got to say, really and truthfully, it's the day an old friend named Jack Cresse called me in Hendersonville, Tennessee to see if I had any interest in getting back into radio. He knew me from several years earlier, when we'd worked together—him in sales and me on the air—at a little radio station in the Tulsa suburb of Sand Springs called KFMJ. Not everybody saw perfectly eye to eye with Jack Cresse, but he liked me and I liked him and we got along good. Other people must've liked him, too, because at the time he got me on the telephone he had recently become KVOO's vice president and general manager.

When we made contact, I was still working for E.T., more or less. But I wasn't going out on the road with him any more. I had become a booking agent with Haze Jones's agency in Hendersonville, lining up dates for Ernest as well as Cal Smith and Jack Greene, two former Texas Troubadours who'd gone on to become stars in their own right.

Why was I booking Ernest instead of singing and playing with his band?

The simple answer is I'd just plain gotten sick of the road.

My first son, Billy Joe, was just a few years old then, hardly more than a baby, and I'd gotten tired of being away from him and Jerri, my wife. Ernest and the Troubadours didn't go out like acts do nowadays, with a few dates over a weekend. We didn't go out for like a Friday and Saturday night, or a Saturday night and Sunday afternoon. When we climbed aboard the Green Hornet, it'd be for seven days, or sometimes 14. I think the longest I was ever on a tour with E.T. was through Texas and California and then on up into Alaska. We were out maybe 21 days that time.

You know what, though? Everything was beautiful. ET was beautiful. Everybody in the band was beautiful. I had no conflicts whatsoever with anybody. But I didn't see any success happening for *me*. I was always too busy on the road to try and do anything in Nashville to help me make it on my own, like Jack and Cal had. I didn't have the time to do anything along those lines. And I missed the home life.

Ernest understood, especially about the family. He had a lot of kids himself. So he got me that job with Haze Jones, right in the town where we were living, and I started booking him and Cal and Jack. E.T. knew we had a nice place in Hendersonville, and that I didn't want to just pick up and leave town in a hurry just after getting off the road. Haze was a nice guy. I didn't make a lot of money, but it was a job, you know?

I didn't like it, though. I didn't like being a booking agent. I wanted to have an agent booking *me*. So I was looking for something else, even if I didn't know exactly what, the day that Jack called.

Like I said earlier, KVOO was a station with a great history. It had become famous as the home of Bob Wills and His Texas Playboys and, later, Johnnie Lee Wills and His Boys; because of Bob's landing at KVOO in 1934 and starting what would be decades of daily broadcasts, KVOO had been the station most responsible for the spread and popularity of the musical mixture that came to be known as western swing, a new kind of sound that included cowboy and what was then called "hillbilly" music, in addition to Dixieland jazz, pop, blues, and Mexican tunes.

But while the Wills brothers and lots of other cowboy-related acts—even Gene Autry—broadcast on KVOO over the years, it was never really considered a "country" station. For several decades before Jack Cresse made his call to me, it had been an affiliate of the NBC network, carrying all kinds of different programs, musical and otherwise.

But when he phoned me that day, he said that was all about to change. Harold Stuart, the lawyer and businessman who owned the station, had been down in Fort Worth, Texas, talking to the owner of another radio station, WBAP, that had just converted to a country-music format. They were doing good, too, especially with an overnight show hosted by one of their deejays, Bill Mack. When Mr. Stuart came back to town, he'd called Jack in and told him, "We're going country." Jack, in turn, remembering our KFMJ days together, called me up and said, "How would you like to be on a 50,000-watt radio station?"

And I said, "I'd love it. Because I'm not diggin' it here."

He offered me any position that I wanted, and I chose the all-night show.

We get into all of that later in the book, but right here I want to come back around to why I think that telephone call was the turning point, the crucial moment, in my public life and my career. Without KVOO, I don't know where I'd be, where I would have gone, what would've happened. Even now, nearly 50 years later, I give KVOO all the credit for whatever Billy Parker is today.

Over the years, some have said that I had a lot to do with what happened to KVOO, 1170 AM, when it became one of the biggest country-music stations on the whole national scene. I appreciate that, but I honestly don't think I had much to do with it. I may have been lucky enough, thanks to Jack Cresse, to come aboard when it first went to a country format, and I may have had some success as a disc jockey as well as a picker and grinner during all my years there, but I sure didn't build the station.

In fact, looking back on it, I believe it was just the opposite. It was the station that built *me*.

> Billy Parker will always be one of the greats . . . whether in person, on radio or stage. Billy is one of the great unsung heroes. Well, we do sing his praises, but we don't sing them as loud or as often as we should. I'm proud that he has this autobiography to really show who he was and is.
>
> With respect,
>
> *Dolly*
>
> DOLLY PARTON

CHAPTER ONE

First of all, don't believe my birth certificate.

I guess you can if you want to, but I wouldn't, because it's wrong—not just once, but twice. It says that a son was born on July 17, 1937, to Lucille and James Parker, and that part's right. But it also says that the birth took place in the Oklahoma town of Okemah, in Okfuskee County. That's the first wrong part. Really, it happened at my folks' home in Tuskegee, 20 miles north, which was even in a different county. I know. I was there.

The closest hospital was in Okemah, so I guess that's why Billie Joe Parker's official birthplace isn't the real one. Yep. *Billie* Joe. That's the second thing the certificate gets wrong. I know that's the way some people spelled the name back then, but I've always spelled it *Billy*.

A lot of the stuff that's happened in my life has been kind of weird. Maybe it all started there at the beginning, when I first came into the world and my birth certificate didn't quite get everything right.

Tuskegee wasn't exactly a big metropolis when I was born, but just about all that's left now is a graveyard. Matter of fact, if you look Tuskegee up on the computer, you'll see that it's officially been named an Oklahoma ghost town. It was better than a ghost town back in the late '30s, when we were there, but the country was still in the Great Depression, and Oklahoma—including Tuskegee—had it even worse with the Dust Bowl. Like a lot of men back then trying to make a living under those circumstances, my dad worked for President Roosevelt's WPA, the Works Progress Administration. He was kind of a farmer, too, but for the WPA he did road work, gravel work, anything that needed to be done. And he was a good worker.

When I was two or three years old, a terrible tornado ripped through Tuskegee. It pretty much tore the town up. Not long after that, we moved up to Bristow, about 30 miles north. I was too young to have much of an idea about what was going on with the family, but the best I remember Dad kept on working for the WPA even after the move.

We stayed in a house there for a few years, Mom and Dad and me and my two older brothers and older sister. Then Dad landed a job with the Douglas Aircraft Company in Tulsa.

I would've been four years old when World War II started, so I still didn't really know what was going on around me to any big extent. But looking back on it, I'm sure that he got the job either just before or right after President Roosevelt declared war, following the Japanese attack on Pearl Harbor on December 7, 1941. Only a few months earlier, Douglas Aircraft had started up out by the Tulsa Municipal Airport, building bombers and other planes, as well as aircraft parts, for the government. My dad found work there, but after a while he switched over to the Spartan Aircraft Company, which was also near the airport, out on Sheridan Avenue, and in addition to building airplanes and parts, he also built those silver-looking travel trailers that were so popular in the '40s and '50s.

We lived for a little while in a place on North Utica Avenue in Tulsa, and then we moved to a two-story apartment building at 1301 North Cincinnati. We lived upstairs—our address was 1301½—and I remember there were two or three other families in the other apartments. It was a little roomier downstairs; at one time, there was even an upholstery shop on the first floor.

This might be a good place to tell you about my family. My oldest brother was James T. Parker, named after our dad. The other brother was Oran Lee Parker, and my sister was Francis Louise Parker. She was the youngest; I came along nine years after her—I'm pretty sure I was an accident—but despite the difference in our ages I was very close to all three.

None of them was what you'd call musical, and neither was my dad, but he loved listening to the *Grand Ole Opry*. Every Saturday night, we'd pick it up out of Nashville on our battery-powered Philco radio. My mom, on the other hand, was a gospel-piano player. We didn't have a piano when we were on North Cincinnati, so she didn't get the opportunity to play very much during those years. But I mean she could really pound those keys when she got the chance. She was Assembly of God, which is how we were all brought up, and those folks love their religious music. Mom sure did. She had played for church services earlier in her life, and in our family's later years in Tulsa, she found another little church to play for.

Although I probably had the performing bug by the time I got to grade school, I don't remember doing any music in the church we attended, down on North Cincinnati. What I *do* recall is setting up under the stairway in the back of our apartment building and holding church services. Children from the neighborhood would come around and I'd read from the Bible and preach a little bit. I don't think I felt called to the ministry or anything like that. Maybe I just wanted to impress the kids.

Some of my closest friends then were the Shouse boys, David and Raymond. There were other Shouses, too, but those are the two names I remember. The whole family lived on Detroit Avenue, just one block over from us, so I knew them from the neighborhood. I think they were a little ahead of me at Emerson Elementary School.

We were all very good friends. I remember that we used to ride our bikes a lot down Utica Avenue, and I know we played some football and stuff like that. One day we were down by the Assembly of God Church, playing a little football on a kind of slope, and I fell and hurt my knee. That was pretty much the end of my football-playing career.

One of the things I did a lot back then was go to the movies. We did it just about every week, mostly on the weekends. Best I remember, it cost a dime. Like a lot of other kids, especially in our part of the country, I loved Roy Rogers and Gene Autry and Hopalong Cassidy, all those cowboy stars. I loved Gene because of his guitar, and I loved Roy because of his guitar and his horse, Trigger. I'd walk down to see their pictures at the Pines Theater at 1514 North Cincinnati, right at the corner of Pine and Cincinnati, which wasn't that long of a trip from my apartment building.

The Pines had a special night, maybe one time a week, when they featured something called Screeno. I think they had it on week nights, which were traditionally slower than weekends; they must've figured they needed something extra to bring in more people on those off-nights, and Screeno must've worked for 'em. It was basically a kind of bingo, with audience members getting cards that gave them chances to win cash or prizes. I remember that I won a rocking chair one night—and I had no way to get it home. Like I said, it wasn't that long of a walk from the theater to our apartment building, but it was sure too far for a kid to carry a rocking chair.

"What in the world am I going to do with this?' I wondered. But the people at the movie house saved it for me, and we got someone to go up and get it and bring it to our building.

My dad or mom couldn't drive down and get it, because we didn't have a car. A lot of the time, they took the bus to get where they were going. Dad rode to his job every weekday with a woman. She'd pick up four or five workers and take them where they needed to be, charging them by the week or the month. Once in a while, a cousin would come by in his old Model A Ford and pick us up. I remember that always being kind of a rough ride, but I guess it was better than no ride at all.

⋆

While I did love those cowboy-movie heroes and their guitars, my heart was always with the performers and music of the *Grand Ole Opry*. Every Saturday night, I'd get out a broomstick that I'd pretend was a guitar and sing along with the *Opry* stars, playing my own version of the air-guitar long before anyone came up with that name. Even when the show wasn't on, no matter where I was or what else I was doing, country music was never very far from my thoughts.

Although my dad had no interest in performing, he was definitely a big fan of what I call real country music, and just about the biggest star in that field at that time was Hank Williams. I remember that the two of us took a cab to see Hank's show one time at the Municipal Theater in downtown Tulsa. (That's the same place that's now known as the Tulsa Theater.) I was still a kid, 11 or 12 years old, so that means that I caught him at a good time, around 1948, not all that long after he'd gotten his MGM Records contract and had become a regular on the Louisiana Hayride radio show out of Shreveport.

I'll never forget that concert. We sat behind one of those big posts that go up the ceiling, and my dad, who was a little guy anyway, would bend over and around with me as we tried to keep our eyes on Hank.

At least we did get to see and hear him. Only a few years after that, Hank got booked into Tulsa's Cain's Ballroom. Mr. O.W. Mayo, who owned the place then, told me much later that ol' Hank had found him some choc beer down the street, and by the time the show was supposed to start he wasn't in any condition to sing. They even tried to prop him up at the mike, but it wasn't any good. Mr. Mayo slipped the bandleader, Blackie Crawford, some extra cash and told him to keep playing and not stop at all for a break. He knew as long as the folks were dancing they would be all right. But if the music quit, people would get to wondering where Hank was and there'd be trouble.

Remember that old joke about the guy who likes both kinds of music: country *and* western? Country music and western music got lumped together years ago, when *Billboard* magazine started using that term for one of the record charts they published. I can tell you it wasn't called "country and western" when I was a kid. A lot of folks just called it "hillbilly" music, while the kinds of songs Roy Rogers and Gene Autry did were known as "cowboy" tunes.

Although they may have seemed a lot alike to people who weren't big fans, they were actually very different. Western music had a kind of Hollywood glow to it; it made you think about the Old West of the movies, which didn't really have a whole lot of relationship to the way things actually were back then. Country music was more earthy, I guess you'd say—it was about real people and their lives and their struggles, the things they laughed about and the things they cried about. It was the music of regular people, folks like us who maybe didn't have a lot but didn't really know we were poor. (In our case, we had folks living around us who were poorer.)

There was a third kind of music I got exposed to during this time. In addition to owning the Cain's, Mr. Mayo was the business manager for Johnnie Lee Wills—and earlier for Johnnie Lee's oldest brother, the famous Bob Wills—and the Cain's was Johnnie Lee's home. In addition to the dances he and his band played for on Thursday and Saturday nights, Johnnie Lee would broadcast noon shows live from the Cain's over KVOO, continuing the tradition started by his brother Bob. The music they played was called western swing. (According to Mr. Mayo, someone—he always said it was Roy Rogers, but I'm not too sure about that—came up with the term "western swing" in the 1940s, when a fellow named Spade Cooley, born in Oklahoma, got big on the West Coast playing pretty much what Bob Wills was playing in Tulsa, dressing his musicians up in western gear. Those were still the big-band pop days, and clarinet player Benny Goodman was known as the King of Swing. Someone then decided to call Spade Cooley the King of *Western* Swing. Anyway, that's how the story goes.)

Much later, in the 1990s, I'd do a western-swing show with one of the co-writers of this book, John Wooley, and we'd talk a lot both on and off the air about what western swing actually was, all of the influences in it and that kind of stuff. We both agreed, and still do, that it had both country music and western music in it, along with a lot of other musical styles like jazz, pop and blues. I know that in the late '40s, standing there in front of the bandstand watching Johnnie Lee Wills and His Boys play, I developed a real fondness for western swing as well as country. Of course, I had no idea at the time that Johnnie Lee would become a great friend of mine or that the two of us would go to Nashville in the early 1980s and cut a couple of songs together with some of the greatest studio musicians who ever hit a lick.

My friend Billy Parker is one of the top-notch promoters of all time. I mean that in a very positive way. Throughout his long impressive tenure at KVOO Radio, Billy never promoted himself. However, being true to his roots, he was a wonderful crusader on behalf of the national country music talent he spun on the air. More importantly to us local guys, he was our staunchest supporter. He never missed an opportunity to enhance and promote our musical efforts. He managed to slip our names in on his shows and mention where we would be performing. When a gig or an event was on your near horizon, you could expect a call to join him live on the air or be invited to tell all about it on **Wooley Wednesday** *or later on his program titled* **Country Junction.**

I spent the night with Billy several times along with the plethora of his listeners to his all night "Big Rigger" slot over KVOO Radio. My job was to help him answer the phone. The calls, from seemingly every 18-wheel driver from all over the country, would overwhelm the KVOO phone lines. Some requested songs, but many just wanted to say "Hi" to the man whose voice, over time, had settled them into what they considered to be the status of Billy's lifelong buddy.

I could go on and on about how Billy, the nationally acclaimed and awarded Disc Jockey, would take his time to meet me at the station at 9:00 pm, waiting on me to come from work, in order for me to cut a new commercial for our western store. He set up annual live broadcasts over KVOO with Johnnie Lee Wills and All The Boys in order to promote our rodeo. Billy never passed up an opportunity to go above and beyond to support us.

My Dad loved to kid Billy. By the way, Dad would only inflict his playful torment on those he was extremely fond of. Billy was always good natured and had plenty of good comebacks of his own. It was fun to hear the good-natured bantering between two friends.

Billy took Dad to Nashville to cut a couple of songs with him for an album he was recording. Their collaboration on "Milk Cow Blues" and "Take Me Back To Tulsa" turned out great. Two months after, Dad passed away. It was very fitting that Dad's last musical endeavor was with his friend Billy Parker.

Billy and I do not visit as much as we probably should. However, every December, without fail, I look forward to my call from Billy, wishing my family and me a very Merry Christmas. We spend phone time getting all caught up.

After knowing Billy for over forty years, I consider him to be a member of the Wills family. I am most proud to claim him as a treasured friend.

~ **JOHN T. WILLS** ~

I spent a lot of time at Cain's Ballroom, both as a fan and as a picker. Johnnie Lee Wills would become one of my best friends.

Me with my first guitar, a Stella.
That's my mom at the piano.

CHAPTER TWO

I did like the guitars those western stars played, and I was crazy about country music, so I guess it was pretty logical for me to start wanting a real instrument for my own. A broomstick was fine for pretending I was on the *Grand Ole Opry* stage with whoever's voice was coming out of our Philco on a Saturday night, but even as a kid I knew there was another step to be taken if I really wanted to perform, and I started wanting real bad to take that step.

Looking back on it, I'm sure that me wanting a guitar had a lot to do with an older cousin of mine named Donald Bryant, who came through Tulsa when I was 10 or 11 and played a gig. It seems like it was at the Cheyenne Lounge. That would've been around 1948 or '49, just a few years after the end of World War II. Both of my brothers had gone off to serve, one in the Army and the other in the Air Force, and they'd gotten back all right and were working in town. My cousin Donald had been in the service, too. I think he still was when he came through, and I believe his branch was the Air Force.

Anyhow, he was a great guitar player, and even though we really never did spend a lot of time together, he impressed me so much that I wanted to be like him. I wanted to play guitar like him.

At around the same time he came through town—I honestly can't tell you if it was before or after—my mom took me down to Rose Pawn on First Street and bought me a used Stella guitar.

A hollow-body guitar didn't cost much in those days, especially when you got it from a pawn shop—and especially when it was a Stella, a brand that was kind of on the low end as far as stringed instruments went. Still, I couldn't have been prouder when I carried it home.

Again, I'm not real sure if I got it before or after my cousin Donald's visit, but I know I bugged her for a good amount of time before we finally made the trip downtown. It's sure possible that Donald, her sister's boy, also had something to do with her decision. Whatever the reasons, I now had a real guitar. No more broomsticks for me. And no more waiting for the Grand Ole Opry when I wanted to sing a country song.

I never got anywhere near as good as Donald Bryant was on the guitar; he could play with the best of 'em. But he was one of the biggest reasons I took it up in the first place. Those cowboy-movie stars and their guitars, along with the country pickers on the Grand Ole Opry, all had something to do with me playing guitar. But they were on the picture-show screens and on the radio; Donald Bryant was a real person, a relative, someone I *knew*. That made a lot of difference.

After Mom bought me the guitar, I remember getting one of those Mel Bay books—Lord knows how many other kids over the years have learned their first chords from ol' Mel—and then, somehow or other, she found a way to pay for some lessons for me at a place called Ernie Scruggs' School of Fine Arts in Tulsa. It was out on either North Boston or North Cincinnati. My teacher was a man named Tex Hoepner, a professional musician who was then in town playing in Al Clauser's band. Clauser was then on the staff of Tulsa radio station KTUL. Among other things, he and his band had a regular show; he gave a young singer named Clara Ann Fowler some of her first work. She'd go on to do all right for herself, especially after changing her name to Patti Page. (Later on, Al had his own record label, Alvera—named after him and his wife, Vera. A lot of my friends would appear on that label.) Al's band was called the Oklahoma Outlaws, and they were western swing through and through. They'd been on the air at the big station WHO in Des Moines and even appeared in a Gene Autry picture called *Rootin' Tootin' Rhythm*, which came out the year I was born. Tex had been in the band for all of that and still was; he played on several recordings for Al and the boys and did their live shows.

Between Tex in person and Mel on the page, I learned the basics well enough to begin accompanying myself on some of the simpler country songs I'd heard. But it would take a few more years before I actually got on the radio. And when I did, it wouldn't be in Nashville, or even in Tulsa—but in a little Oklahoma town with one radio station, and a local personality on that station who decided to give a young teenager a chance to sing into a microphone.

In the early '50s, I was living with my folks in a house at 2639 E. Haskell Street in Tulsa, east of where we'd lived before, and going to school at Grover Cleveland Junior High. My sister and two brothers were long gone by this time, all three of them out doing their own thing. I didn't know it at the time, but pretty soon I'd be doing the same. Halfway through my freshman year, in early 1952, I dropped out. I was 14 years old.

The reason I left home—and school—had a lot to do with my mom and dad getting divorced. She left and went her way, and Dad and I stayed in the house on Haskell Street. I won't say I went to hell in a handbasket after that, and I know a lot of kids go through plenty worse than I had it in those days, but it sure changed my life around. It was just kind of a bad situation. So, midway through my ninth-grade year, instead of returning to school, I caught a bus in Tulsa—Dad bought my ticket—and headed for the town of McAlester, about 100 miles south of Tulsa. My sister and her husband, who was an ironworker, had a job there. They met me at the bus station, and I went to live with them.

It was in a room in their house that I started playing deejay for the first time. I remember having two record players there, and I'd play a song, read a commercial out of a magazine, and play another song. (These were the days of the big 78 rpm records.) I'd be in there talking up a storm, doing sell jobs for all these different products, and they'd be in the next room, laughing at me.

While I remember playing disc jockey a lot, I don't recall exactly how it was I got up the nerve to go to the local radio station, KNED, and see if maybe they'd put me on the air. But I do know that one day I grabbed up my guitar and walked to the Aldridge Hotel, which housed the KNED studio, and got in to see a local radio celebrity named Carl Garnand, who sang on the station. His dad was a guard at the Oklahoma State Penitentiary there in McAlester.

I knew I wasn't good enough to be on the air myself, but I just wanted it bad enough to try. And pretty soon, I'd made it. I was playing with Carl Garnand, strumming along as he sang "I'm Movin' On," doing 30 minutes every weekday afternoon and 15 minutes on Saturday mornings. In those days, a local radio station had a lot of impact in the surrounding areas, and pretty soon I was going around with Carl playing live shows in little towns like Checotah and Eufaula. These weren't club jobs. They were usually school-auditorium-type things. He'd work the dates and I'd go along and play guitar behind him. I don't think I ever got one check from the radio station for playing over the air, but I remember Carl would give me a few bucks whenever we did a show together.

Of course, I was still a kid, and I wasn't making a living or anything like that with my music. But going on the radio and going out with Carl helped me decide that's what I wanted to do with my life. I think that's when I really decided that I was going to be both a performer and a deejay.

It did work out that way. But not for a while.

Publicity photo from around 1952
on KNED radio in McAlester, Oklahoma.

CHAPTER THREE

I'm not sure exactly how long I stayed in McAlester with my sister and brother-in-law, but it couldn't have been more than a year or two. I believe I was somewhere around 16 when I came back to Tulsa, which would make it in the neighborhood of 1953. Once I returned, I split my time between living with my dad on Haskell Street and staying at my mom's. Although Dad had stayed single, Mom had remarried, and she and her new husband had a place in Oakhurst, just west of the city, out near the Turner Turnpike gate. They had a shed out back of their house, and it wasn't long before I'd gotten a record player set up out there so I could keep on playing at being a disc jockey. By this time, I knew—and so did the rest of the family—that radio and entertaining were in my blood.

Even though I had a little experience playing on KNED back in McAlester, I didn't really have any kind of an idea about how to break into the business and actually make a living at it. That's what I would've loved to have done—if I'd known how. What I *did* know was this: Since I wasn't going to school, I'd better find me some kind of a job. So I did. It was with the J.D. Young Company, which is still around and doing great. I started working for them as a delivery boy, taking photostats around town to different businesses. At the time, J.D. Young did printing and binding and stuff like that, and a big part of what they did then was make copies of blueprints and things like that. It may be hard for people today to think of a world without copy machines, there wasn't a one of 'em anywhere until the first Xerox copier started showing up in about 1960. Before that, businesses depended on companies like J.D. Young to make photostatic copies for them.

I think I began at a couple of places called the Tulsa Camera Record and Triangle Blueprint before going to J.D. Young, but I know that what I did was ride my bike all over Tulsa, delivering photostats and blueprints. After I got my driver's license, the company trusted me enough to let me use one of their trucks to make deliveries, and it was a big day on the job when I got to trade in two wheels and pedals for four wheels and a motor.

Over the months I worked for J.D. Young, I got to know downtown Tulsa pretty well, riding through it and going into offices in all those buildings. One of the places I got to know the best didn't have anything to do with my day job, though. It was around this time, maybe when I was 17 or 18, that I got a little after-hours gig playing at a beer joint called the Springdale Tavern, over on Pine and Lewis.

I kept my day job, as the old saying goes, and eventually I went from delivering photostats for J.D. Young to actually making them on a machine. But while I was doing that on weekdays, I was also playing Friday and Saturday nights at the Springdale Tavern.

Even though I've tried as hard as I can to remember the circumstances that led me to that particular place, I just can't come up with anything. I can't give the credit (or blame) to my folks. Dad never drank a drop in his life, and my mama didn't either, so they wouldn't have been hanging out at a place like that. It could be that someone I knew, maybe someone I was doing a little pickin' with, got me in. The best I can recall, I started out playing there as a solo act. I think I chiseled myself in to a certain extent, because I wasn't a good guitar player then. I never was, really. But I sold 'em and started playing there on the weekends.

I don't know how long it was just me, but pretty soon I picked up an accordion player named Bob Johnson and his brother Al, who played bass. So the kitty, which was all we got for playing, would be split three ways—sometimes more, when people sat in with us. We'd get some good musicians coming by, too. It's during that time in my life that I started getting to know a lot of the boys in Johnnie Lee Wills's band. Johnnie Lee was at the Cain's Ballroom and broadcasting over KVOO then. He'd been doing that since his oldest brother Bob had left for the service in '43, and while Bob didn't last too long in the military—their sister Lorene always said that Bob and the army just didn't get along—he'd gone on to California and Texas and left Johnnie Lee to take care of things in Tulsa.

I remember Leon Rausch sitting in with us some during those weekends. Of course, Leon would go on to a great career with Bob and the band that was formed after Bob died, the Original Texas

Playboys. And there were so many others—Ted Haff, a great fiddler and singer, and Tommy Elliot, the steel-guitar player and singer who wrote the song "Sold Out, Doc," which he'd recorded with Johnnie Lee for RCA Victor a few years earlier. I played "Sold Out, Doc" with him many times at the Springdale Tavern.

There was a place next door where we all liked to eat. It had the best Coney Islands in the world. You could get a beer and a Coney Island there, and that made a pretty good dinner. I also remember a bar down on Pine Street called Ed & Irene's. It was a rough place, and when they moved around the corner and set up a new establishment, it was just as bad as the old one. I played some for 'em, though. I'd sit in with different people—Gene Mooney, Ted Creekmore, Johnny Stills—all these guys who had country bands going in Tulsa back in the mid-'50s.

To tell you the truth, I was spending a lot of my time in clubs back in those days, even though I wasn't even old enough to drink—legally, that is. When I look back on those years, I realize that I was leading a pretty rough life.

★

By 1955, the year I turned 18, my music career wasn't exactly taking off like a rocket, but I was at least getting some new places to pick and grin. Bob Duvall, who played steel guitar, and I got to where we were playing pretty regularly on KOTV, Channel 6, which was the main station in Tulsa at the time. It was just the two of us, Bob and me, and I remember that Betty Boyd, the Tulsa TV pioneer who'd get to be my good friend, and Bob Latting, who not only emceed shows but also owned the Golden Drumstick restaurant (in the building that had once been home to the Casa Del Club, where a lot of the early Tulsa rock 'n' rollers played), were two of the people we worked with the most. Bob Latting had a Saturday afternoon show called *Kids Carnival*, which brought in a lot of young musicians, and I think that was the show we did kind of regularly.

Local television was a lot bigger deal in those days, and a lot of people started recognizing me just from those little gigs we were doing on Channel 6. That may be how I first got acquainted with Marijohn Wilkin; her husband, Art; and their son, Bucky. On the other hand, I kind of remember working some dates with Bucky. I think Bob Duvall and I played with him somewhere—maybe Pryor, Oklahoma—and it could be that I got to know the Wilkins that way.

Later on, Bucky would become a rock 'n' roll recording star, fronting Ronny and the Daytonas, the only surf- and hot-rod-music band I know of that was based in Nashville. They had big pop hits in the '60s with "Little Honda" and "Sandy." And his mother would go on to be a well-known country-music songwriter. Her most famous tune was probably the one she wrote with Kris Kristofferson, "One Day at A Time," but she had lots of other big country songs, like "Waterloo," "Long Black Veil," and Jimmy Dean's "P.T. 109."

At the time I got acquainted with the family, Bucky was still a kid, maybe 10 years younger than me, and Marijohn was just getting started with her songwriting career. She was writing with a guy named James P. Coleman, and she and Coleman got connected with the great country star Red Foley, who was then hosting a radio and TV show out of Springfield, Missouri called *The Ozark Jubilee*. In January of 1955, it got picked up by ABC-TV for a weekly broadcast, which made it one of the first country-music television shows to run regularly on a national network.

Red Foley was one of the top stars in the business at that time, and lots of other big names—or people who would *become* big names—were in the cast: Porter Wagoner, Wanda Jackson, Leroy Van Dyke, Carl Smith, Sonny James, Jean Shepherd, Webb Pierce, Marvin Rainwater, Brenda Lee (who wasn't even a teenager then), and more. Plus, they brought in lots of recording artists as guest stars.

Although I didn't know it then—heck, I was 18, and I didn't know much of anything—there was a big push on at the time to make Springfield and not Nashville the country-music capital of the world. A couple of radio guys, Ralph Foster and Si Siman, were behind that deal; in 1953, they'd started *The Ozark Jubilee* on a local TV station; the next year, they got Red to host it. Then, the third year, 1955, ABC-TV picked it up. Pretty soon, Springfield had a talent agency and a song-publishing company, and more and more artists started moving there. In 1955, it was a happenin' place, with Red and *The Ozark Jubilee* anchoring the whole dang thing. Millions of people from all over watched or listened to the show, and Red and many other artists used it to help get audiences out to see them when they went on tour.

How does this fit in with the Wilkins and me? Marijohn was one of the artists who moved there, along with Bucky and Art. And not long after they left Tulsa for Springfield, they invited me to come up. For someone who loved country music, it sounded like the place to be. So I went.

⋆

I always thought that Marijohn moved the family to Missouri because she had a Springfield connection through the guy she was writing songs with, James P. Coleman. He'd been hired to handle publicity and promotion for Red Foley. I still believe that's a big reason why the Wilkins went, and I know that Art, who wasn't in the music business, got some sort of a job after they settled there. But since then, I've read that the Wilkins made the move so that Bucky could appear on *The Junior Jubilee*, which was a kids' showcase broadcast once a month in place of the regular *Ozark Jubilee*. Brenda Lee got her start on that show, and Bucky sure enough got on it as well, playing guitar. Meanwhile, Marijohn was writing songs with Coleman that started getting cut by other members of the *Ozark Jubilee* cast, and she sang a little bit around town and went on the road as part of Red Foley's tour.

That's where I came in. After I moved to Springfield, James P. Coleman—who was Red's publicity man, you remember—gave me a job doing advance phone sales for the Red Foley touring shows. It was one of those boiler-room deals that they don't do as much today, although they still do it some. This is how it worked: A group in each city where Red was scheduled to play would sponsor the show. It could be the local sheriffs' department, the Fraternal Order of Police, the Shriners—organizations like that. Whoever sponsored it would furnish a room for making calls, and there'd be three or four of us, each on a phone. We'd all get a list of people to call up, different businesses like tire places and automobile dealerships—I think we even called residences—and we'd try to sell tickets and advertising for the program book that would be at the show. We'd try and get whoever was on the other end all pumped up about the show, telling 'em, "It's gonna be a barnburner," that kind of b.s. We'd also make sure they knew that part of the proceeds went to the Fraternal Order of Police, or whoever it was, and then ask how many tickets they wanted. The tactics were a little bit high-pressure, I guess, but it worked and we filled up a lot of auditoriums for Red's shows.

I don't know that I ever made any real money hawking those tickets. I may have made a little, but I don't think it was much. Money wasn't really what I was after anyway. My own payoff came during the concert itself, when I'd get to come on stage and sing a song or two with Red and his band.

I was the only one, I think, who got paid that way. The rest of the guys on those boiler-room operations were mostly drinkers and promoters, if you know what I mean; they weren't interested in show business the way I was. And while it's been an awful long time, I can still remember getting up under the spotlight with Red, hearing him introduce me to that big crowd, and then going to the microphone and doing a song or two. He'd pat me on the shoulder or on the head and call me "son." Then that show'd be over and we'd go on down the line.

Red and his wife, Sally, both treated me nice, but I didn't see them very often. For one thing, I didn't work all of his shows. I worked *some* of 'em, but I had to make a living, too, so I had a lot of outside jobs. A lot of times they were in grocery stores. I spent a lot of days stocking shelves and delivering groceries. In fact, that's what I did *after* I left Red Foley. I was still doing it when I got my first real disc-jockey job.

I know it's hard to believe, but that first time I worked as a deejay, it wasn't on a country station, or even a pop or rock 'n' roll station. My disc-jockey career began in Colorado—at a classical music station!

Early publicity photo of me from the late 1950s.

CHAPTER FOUR

Springfield may have threatened Nashville for a year or two when it came to dominance in country music, but that big push ran out of steam in the late '50s and Nashville rose to the top again.

That's where Marijohn and her family went after a couple of years in Missouri, and she and Bucky both went on to have a lot of success. I'm happy for 'em, and I'll always be grateful for their help in getting me a little closer to a career in the business. Marijohn introduced me to people like Stan Hitchcock, who was a country artist then. In the early '90s, about 35 years after I met him (at the Corn Crib Restaurant in Springfield), he became the head of the Americana Television Network in Branson, Missouri, and hired me to do a bunch of TV shows for him.

The Wilkins were just very kind to me. Later on, when I got established on the air, I made a point of playing a lot of the songs she'd written for different people, but I know she and Art did more for me than I've ever done for them.

If you're wondering what all this has to do with my first disc-jockey job, it's this: The Wilkins introduced me to Red Foley, and it was through promoting Red's shows that I got to Englewood, Colorado, where I was living when I became, if only for a little bit, a deejay on a classical station. Red was playing in an auditorium up there—I think it was a big school auditorium—and he had me come up and sing with him that night. That same evening, I met a young woman named Vereen Ann Brianza. When Red and the show moved on, I stayed, and Vereen and I got married not long afterwards. This was in 1957; I was 20 years old.

Once I left Red Foley, I played a few things around the Englewood area, but I really didn't do too much music-wise. I got a job at the Shop Rite supermarket in Englewood, delivering groceries, stocking shelves, and doing just about anything else that needed to be done. It was the kind of day job I was used to. But the little taste of entertaining people I'd gotten with Red and even before, with Carl Garnand in McAlester and KOTV in Tulsa—not to mention the club jobs—stayed with me. I still knew I wanted to be an entertainer, whether over the radio or on stage, but I still didn't know quite how to go about it.

Then, one day, I saw a little ad in the local newspaper about a station in Golden, Colorado, needing a disc jockey. Golden, the home of Coors beer, was only about 20 miles northwest of Englewood, so I drove up there and applied. At the time, you had to have an FCC license to be a deejay, and I took the test for the entry-level license, Class C, and passed. That got me the job of weekend announcer on a classical-music station.

As you might have guessed, I didn't hold onto it long—maybe a month. I mean, hell, I was *country*, not classical. I could read and all, even though I only had eight and a half years of school, but I know some of my pronunciations weren't right. Still, there are things in your life that you do just to get by, and that job at least got me started. I learned how to work with turntables and that kind of thing, so that alone was worth the 20 bucks it cost me to get that FCC license. I'm still holding onto it, in fact. Who knows? I might need it again someday.

When you get to be my age, there are a lot of things you can't remember. There are also some things you don't *want* to remember. One of those is my first marriage. It didn't work. By the end of 1959, it was over, but it had been unraveling long before that. Even our two baby girls, Elizabeth and Kathy, weren't enough to keep the marriage together.

Both of our girls had been born at St. Francis hospital in Tulsa, which tells you that we—and sometimes, just me—had been going back and forth between Tulsa and Colorado. My mom loved the kids, and we usually stayed with her out in Oakhurst when we were in Tulsa.

But Vereen never liked it in Oklahoma. At no time did she ever want to make Tulsa her home. Of course, I did, and that was just one more strain on the marriage. It all came to a head when I took the girls to Tulsa with me and Vereen stayed behind in Colorado. I won't get into what was going on then. I'll just say I don't really think she was a bad mother. But she wasn't a very responsible person, either, and I finally thought it would be best for the girls if they were raised by my own family and me.

Vereen's mother and father didn't agree. They came to Tulsa, sued me for custody of Kathy and Elizabeth, and won. So both of the babies had to go back to Colorado. When that happened, it just about broke my mom's heart, and it didn't do me any good, either.

I didn't see my girls again until they were grown.

Back in Tulsa, I started back in doing what I'd done before I left—playing in clubs and around, mostly on weekends, and holding down a regular job as well. I booked out mostly as a single, working with house bands around town whenever I could. I *think* that Bob and Al Johnson and I got back in the Springdale Tavern then, at least on Saturdays. I remember how everybody used to come out there, all the musicians, after one of Johnnie Lee Wills's Saturday night dances at the Cain's.

The regular job I had was with QuikTrip. Of course, that chain of stores—which began in Tulsa in '58—has thousands of locations all over the world now. Back then, though, there were only a few. As a matter of fact, when I first started with 'em, there were three stores, all in Tulsa, two on Peoria and another one out on Pine. Soon, there was a bunch more. (No one called them "convenience stores"; that title hadn't come along yet. And the products they sold were a little different. They stocked a lot of canned goods, and they didn't even sell gas.)

There were only two positions at QuikTrip then: manager, and assistant manager. I can truthfully say I was both at one time or another. So can my brother Oran, who followed me into that business. (Jim, our oldest brother, was an electrician.)

I might've made a career out of QuikTrip if I hadn't still been pestered by the microphone bug. The company treated me good and I didn't have any complaints. But one night, when I was mopping up at the end of my shift at QuikTrip No. 6, over on North Main, I heard an announcer say that the station was looking for a part-time weekend deejay.

This time, thankfully, it wasn't a classical station. It was KFMJ, which had religious programming in the morning and pure-dee country music for the rest of the day.

I'm not going to tell you that I threw down the mop and bolted out of the store to try and get that job, but I may have felt like it. Finally, maybe, I'd have the chance to be on the air again. And this time, I'd be able to play the music that I loved—real, honest country, the kind I'd grown up on.

It wasn't long before I'd set up an interview with KFMJ's station manager, Ron Blue. I still had the little FCC license I'd gotten in Colorado, and that may have helped. Maybe my experience doing those Channel 6 TV shows and the little time I'd had as a classical-music-station announcer didn't hurt, either. Whatever the reasons, he hired me on the spot, and I started out part-time on Saturdays, just putting in tapes and that kind of stuff—what radio people call working the board. Ron Blue gave me the opportunity to have my own Saturday show, too, but there was one provision. I had to sell all the advertising for it. The spots cost 10 dollars each, and there were 10 spots. So I had to sell $100 worth of advertising in order to be able to do the show.

Best I remember, it was called *The Broken Arrow Hour*, which meant that all the advertisers had to cater to the people in that Tulsa suburb. I wasn't from Broken Arrow, so I don't know whose idea it was for me to do a show with that name. I'm thinking maybe it was a guy named Hank Stanford, who was already there, working as both a deejay and a salesman, just like I was doing.

It seems like from the beginning of my radio career, it was always, "if you can sell it, you can have it." So, honestly, what I did was sell myself into radio. I went out and sold those spots to different advertisers, pocketed 10 or 15 percent of the money—10 or 15 bucks—and took to the airwaves on a fully sponsored program.

I also got a little help from a guy who was on the station. The name he used was Johnny Western, but I want to make sure you know this wasn't my friend Johnny Western who sang, wrote songs, and had a hall of fame career as a country-music deejay over Wichita's KFDI. This was a different guy.

One day, only a couple of weeks after I'd started at KFMJ, this Johnny Western didn't show up for his shift. They called me in at the spur of the moment to do his show, and I guess I did it well enough that they gave me his slot on the air. So, with that show and *The Broken Arrow Hour*, I had my foot in the door pretty good. I was making enough money to get by as an employee of KFMJ, and

I was also making a few bucks pickin' and grinnin' around town.

I guess all that playing radio I'd done at my sister's place when I was a kid, and later on in the shed back of my mom's house, finally paid off. That's how I felt at the time, anyway. I was glad to have a radio home that would give me a chance to bring real country music to folks—and maybe help me do a little bit of my own, too.

I have spent my long life in the pursuit of musical entertainment in all its various forms, and in so doing, I've gotten to know the citizens of this strange and exotic world of show-biz. You may wonder, away from the spotlights, curtains, stage clothes and raw energy of performance...what is the "real" person like? Strip away that fantasy persona that we exhibit to the crowds, TV cameras and the microphones...are we real, fake or somewhere in-between? Well, in country music, most are real, true- blue down-to-earth folks, and we stay that way because country music fans can spot a "fake" in no time.

However, there are degrees of "real," and let me share with you the finest example of "true-blueism" that I have come to know in this circus of music.

I first met Billy Parker when he came to Nashville to appear on my television show, and we became "brothers of song." I call us brothers, because "friend" is not descriptive enough. We all have good friends, but to call one a "brother of song"...well, that is a special category enjoyed by only a few.

Billy has had a dual career in music...as a performer/ recording artist, and as a top country music disc jockey on

THANKS—THANKS A LOT

Tulsa's Radio giant, KVOO. Billy is a pioneer in country music late-night radio and prime-time daytime radio. Artists, on tour in the early years, would take a detour to Tulsa to come to the station and sit with Billy, drinking his coffee and telling stories...for no other reason than that they loved Billy Parker.

Now, there is a dang good reason for one man to gain the love and respect of so many. Billy Parker is simply the finest and truest friend a "picker" could ever have. If you are sick Billy will be calling to say, "Hey, are you doing okay? What do you need?"...and you know he means it. Billy and I have been prayer partners for years, because that is what special friends do. Billy and I have laughed together, worked together, shared secrets that no one else will ever know, and we have cried together at the loss of good friends.

Yeah, Billy Parker is "real" all right. He hasn't got a false bone in his old country self. I love you Billy. You are a friend to walk the high trails with.

~ **STAN HITCHCOCK** ~

CHAPTER FIVE

KFMJ, my first real radio home, had started out back in the late 1940s as a network affiliate, like most of the stations were back then, with national radio shows and news and some local programming. The first owner was Fred Jones, who was real famous around Tulsa for a long time as one of the town's top car dealers. People still remember Fred Jones Ford. His station's call letters stood for the names of him and his wife—Fred and Mary Jones.

My buddy Wayne McCombs, who knows as much about Tulsa radio history as anybody, says that the station went to the gospel and country format in the late '50s. On the *Tulsa TV Memories* website (tulsatvmemories.com) not too long ago, he wrote, "Billy Parker, Jay Jones, and Will Jones, three KFMJ disc jockeys from the late '50s to the late '60s, became Tulsa radio legends. In the '70s and '80s, they made KVOO one of the top country music stations in the nation. Another popular announcer was David Ingles, who now owns KYND and KDIM radio in Tulsa."

I don't know about that "legend" stuff, especially when it comes to me, but we did have some awful good announcers and deejays at KFMJ. And after the weekday-morning gospel and on weekends, we were able to bring people a whole lot of true country music.

According to Wayne's website story, KFMJ had signed on in 1946, and Fred Jones kept it until 1960. The new owner was a man from Oklahoma City named Frank Lynch, who had it when I first went to work there. Frank and his son Mike ran the station for about three years before they sold it to the televangelist Oral Roberts, who, Wayne wrote, "kept the station preaching/teaching in the morning and country the remainder of the day."

That was in 1963. Frank and Mike went on to buy KFDI in Wichita, Kansas, moving up there to take over the station. (They'd both come into my life again many years later, when they and their partner "Ol' Mike" Oatman—a great salesman and air personality from El Paso, Texas who joined them at KFDI—had Great Empire Broadcasting. That was the company that owned KVOO, and several other country stations, throughout most of the 1990s. They were good folks.)

Of course, Oral Roberts, who took over KFMJ from the Lynches, was one of the city's most famous citizens, a big-time preacher who was especially known for his healing ministry. During the time that he owned KFMJ, word got around that the call letters stood for Keep Feeding Me Jesus—which of course wasn't true..

Even though the station changed hands, I managed to stay on, and so did a lot of others, including station manager Ron Blue, the man who'd hired me.

Since KFMJ was really the place that launched my radio career, I had a lot of "firsts" there. As I said earlier, I'd had to sell advertising from the beginning in addition to being a deejay, so KFMJ was where I began my association with a lot of Tulsa businesses. The very first one I remember was Reeves TV and Appliances. David Ingles and I wrote the jingle that Flint Reeves used for years and years, the one that went, "If you didn't buy at Reeves, you paid too much."

A couple of other big things happened during those early years at KFMJ. I met and became acquainted with Ray Bingham, who would not only become my great friend but my manager and booking agent as well. And I would get into recording as well as playing and singing, cutting a song that would become one of the top country hits of the 1960s.

Unfortunately for me, it wouldn't be my version that hit. But it would nevertheless be a record that would turn out to have a huge effect on my career and life.

The first records I ever had out were released by a man named Pappy Daily down in Houston. He was quite a guy, and a pretty big figure in country music. In the early '50s, he'd been one of the people who started a new label, Starday, out of Texas, and that's where George Jones got started. In fact, Pappy was the guy who helped George break into the big time. In the early '60s, he was a producer at both Mercury Records and Starday, and then became the country-music director for the United Artists label. Since I was at KFMJ then, I was playing some of the stuff he was associated with, and I'm sure that's how I got to know him.

Around that same time, he came up with Big D Records, which, as I understand it, concentrated mostly on acts from in and around Texas. Oklahoma was pretty well represented on the roster, with folks like Merl Lindsay, the western-swing bandleader from Oklahoma City, and Merle Kilgore in there with the likes of Texans Willie Nelson (real early in his career, of course) and the Big Bopper.

Brett and John and I have been relying on a couple of good websites—*Discogs* (www.discogs.com) and *45cat* (www.45cat.com)—to fill in the blanks in my memory when it comes to the records I've done, and they've been a big help. In fact, the 45cat site even gives exact dates of release for my D Records 45s—December 29, 1961 for "Dark As the Night" b/w (backed with) "Out of Your Heart," and May 26, 1962 for "Unexpected Heartaches b/w "Almost Gone." I wrote all of those but "Almost Gone," which is credited to Garold Gay. As I recall it, I cut the songs in Tulsa and sent the tapes to Pappy Daily. For the life of me, though I can't remember which studio I used.

Neither one of those singles did anything much, but they were my first, and I think at the time they seemed like another step up the ladder. And now that I look back on it, it's possible Pappy may have inspired me to start up a label myself.

A little later, we'll get to the singles I did for a couple of other labels after Big D, but I want to jump ahead right now to the middle of the '60s, when I began recording not only my own stuff, but other people's as well. It was mostly done for a label I named Pride Records. (There were several little local labels around the area then. David Ingles, for instance, my compadre at KFMJ, recorded some people—including me—on a label called Mr. Music.) It was a *lot* harder to get anything recorded then than it is now, where you can put together a whole CD, from recording to packaging, with a computer in your bedroom, you know. Back then, you or whoever was doing the financing had to get your pickers together in a studio, hire an engineer to get it all right, have a master made, and then get it pressed on vinyl. After all that, you had to go out and try and sell it and get deejays to play it.

For a long time now, I've thought Pride Records was pretty much the definition of "short-lived." When Brett and John asked me about it, I told 'em that having Pride Records helped me learn more about production, and engineering, and even songwriting, even though I suspected it had only been around for a few months at the most. But then John showed me a book he had about Tulsa rock 'n' rollers from the '50s through the mid-'70s. It's Volume Two of the *Oklahoma Guide to 45 rpm Records & Bands*, written by Teb Blackwell and Rhett Lake. They're a couple of big-time record collectors and experts on Oklahoma music, and, according to them, a total of 48 singles came out on my label, which I find kind of hard to believe. But I sure can't argue with their research.

The authors of the book listed me as having the first Pride Records single, "Sing Me A Sad Song" backed with "It Takes A Lot of Money," and an artist called Laura Boring with the last one "Big D" and "Don't Ever." In between, there's a whole bunch of country and rock 'n' roll acts. Some—like Johnny Stills, Benny Ketchum, and Ted Creekmore—I remember very well. Others ring faint bells, and a few I just can't recall.

I do remember that I was writing some then, and a couple of the tunes I'd recorded were ones I'd written. (According to the *Oklahoma Guide*, I only released two singles of my own on the label.) Other people cut my songs, too. I remember Ron Chandler, a good entertainer who played for decades around Tulsa, recording one of mine for Pride Records called "I Discovered You." It got some local airplay, too—but most of it was on KFMJ, and that was because I was doing my own playlists.

My pal Ray Bingham was managing several Tulsa acts at the time—including me—and he said that one of his singers, Austin Maxey, accused him for a long time of stealing the royalties from the record I did on him. Of course, there weren't any royalties, and after Maxey finally understood the business a little better, he apologized to Ray.

The records Ron Chandler and Austin Maxey cut, if I remember right, were country. But I also remember recording some rock 'n' roll acts, too. There was a group called The Band—Gordon Shryock was the guy from that group who made the record deal with me. He was still a teenager when I took him out to KVOO, home to one of the few real recording studios in town, where my pal Jack Moore was the engineer. (I think Mo Billington, the great piano player for Leon McAuliffe, was doing some of the engineering, too. I know he was working with KVOO in some capacity then.) Gordon turned out to be one of the many guys from Tulsa who made a big impression on the national rock scene; he even won some Grammys for engineering gospel records by Andrae Crouch and Reba Rambo.

The Oklahoma Guide says the band that recorded the Pride single was Shryock on guitar, Don Quick on drums, Don's brother Paul Quick on bass, and Larry Bell on piano and vocals. Bell had written what would be the A-side, "Mr. Guitar Man," with fellow Tulsa musician Johnny Cale, who'd later go on to fame as J.J. Cale.

Here's what the *Oklahoma Guide* writers had to say about the record:

> Bell blew the dust off of it [the song] and he and Shryock put together a group of top-rate Tulsa musicians and recorded the track at KVOO radio studios with Billy Parker mixing it. . . . They had not planned a B-side, so they recorded an old Billy Parker tune, 'The Lovin' Zone,' for the flip. Parker's Tulsa label, Pride Records, pressed 1,000 copies, and the A-side was an immediate hit in the Tulsa area drawing the attention of the Nashville label Tener Records, who took it to a regional hit that topped at #2 and #1 on several radio stations including Tulsa's KAKC and KELi respectively in 1965.

I hate to sound like Austin Maxey, but I don't remember ever getting any royalties for writing the B-side. I guess it's too late now—for me and Austin both.

Another Pride Records rock act was the Rogues Five; the A-side of their single was called "It's on Again," the B-side "Too Good for Love." In the *Oklahoma Guide*, one of their guitarists, George

Thomas, called it "that silly record [made in] the summer of 1966." I guess it was silly; I don't know. I do know that the Rogues Five were a big rock band around Tulsa for a couple of years, with my buddy I.J. Ganem singing lead. He went on to a long career, including some time as a headliner in Branson, Missouri, and his guitarist buddy in the Rogues Five, Randy Ess, has also had a long career in the Tulsa area. The band's drummer, Jamie Oldaker, made a name for himself with some of the biggest rock acts of the '70s, guys like Eric Clapton and Peter Frampton.

One of the rock 'n' roll guys I produced would later become a big name in the country realm. He was Mel McDaniel, the Checotah native who grew up in Okmulgee and had those great hits in the '80s like "Baby's Got Her Blue Jeans On," "Louisiana Saturday Night." and "Stand Up." I played ol' Mel a lot then and had him on my shows several times. He and his songs were real popular, and he was a good guy.

Back then, though, in the early '60s, Mel was just a kid. That's when he did a record with me and Pride.

In 1986, when my co-author John Wooley was working as the country-music writer for the *Tulsa World*, he talked to Mel about the record we did together. In the March 28 edition of the paper, John told his readers that Mel and I had first met in 1964, "when McDaniel and a group of Tulsa musicians that included Johnny (later to gain fame as JJ) Cale trouped into the KVOO studios to cut a Cale-penned song called 'Lazy Me.'"

Mel told Wooley: "You've got to start somewhere, you know. Through some friends or something, Johnny's name had come up, so

I went over to his house and said, 'Johnny, I want to make a record.' He played me several songs and one of them was 'Lazy Me.'"

For my part of the story, I remembered that the record was "on a black label" and that I played it on the air. "Mel's record was a country song," I told John, "although back then it might've been considered a little rocky."

Going back to Teb Blackwell's book, though, I can't find "Lazy Me" anywhere in the Pride Records listing—by Mel or anybody else. There *is* a Mel McDaniel single, though, "College Man" b/w "This Heart of Mine," so maybe both Mel and I just misremembered the title. Or it might have been that I helped with the "Lazy Me" recording, and someone else, like David Ingles and Mr. Music Records, actually released it.

Before I leave the rockers, I ought to mention the Cinders, who are also covered in the *Oklahoma Guide*. Keats Tyler, who was a guitarist with the group, said in an interview for the book that "one day in 1965" they decided they should cut a record and went to the KVOO studios where they ran into me. "It turned out that we actually auditioned for Parker, he liked what he heard and told us to write some more songs, then come back to see him."

Keats said that I ended up managing them for a while, getting them into some bigger gigs as well as recording two singles on 'em. I'm glad they thought I was helpful to them and what they were trying to accomplish.

There are other non-country-sounding acts on that Pride Records list—the Preachers, the Rompers, and some band called Group Love Corp. (I guess I ought to remember *them*, hadn't I?) But there's been too much water under the bridge. I have no idea how I got the opportunity to work with any of the rock 'n' rollers, unless it was like what Keats Tyler said, that they sought *me* out for some reason. To be real honest, I didn't really dig the whole rock scene. I was a country guy. But in those days, you'd do a lot of different things hoping that something might hit. You just wanted to get something going.

It's possible that some of the rockers and I got acquainted, at least in part, because of a Saturday afternoon show I started doing with the man I've mentioned earlier, my good, good friend Ray Bingham.

Like me, Ray was eaten up with country music. He especially loved western swing, which had really gotten popular in the 1930s and '40s, with a big reason being Bob Wills's broadcasts over KVOO from the Cain's Ballroom. Bob's brother Johnnie Lee Wills had kept up the weekday shows until 1959, and then he and Bob had gone off to play in Las Vegas. (Johnnie Lee's home would always be Tulsa, but he and his group never were the Cain's house band after they left.)

That first famous group of Bob Wills' Texas Playboys, like so many other bands, was broken up by World War II. After the war, Bob's well-known steel-guitarist Leon McAuliffe had returned from teaching flying to Navy aviators down in Norman, Oklahoma, and set up his own place, the Cimarron Ballroom, which had been the Akdar Shrine Temple in downtown Tulsa. At the time we got acquainted, Ray was the owner of a good business, Clark's Upholstery and Drapery in Tulsa. But, as I said, he'd been bitten by the country-music bug and had gotten into a second job booking bands. He'd bring acts into the Cimarron when Leon and his Cimarron Boys were out on tour, and he also was working with a real good entertainer in Tulsa named Frances Self and her band, the Playmates.

Like I said, back then we were trying a lot of different things to see what might work, and according to Ray, one of the things we tried was a live sock hop from the Cimarron on Saturday afternoons, where he spun records and kids could come in and dance for free. I remember helping Ray get that Saturday afternoon show, but I don't remember much of anything about the sock hops. Ray says that they didn't last very long, maybe four months, and that we played Elvis records and once had a live band, Rodney and the Blazers, a big act from the area. (Rodney was Rodney Lay, who later led Roy Clark's band for more than 20 years and had his own solo records as a country-music recording act. These days, he's playing western swing as a bassist and vocalist with the Tulsa Playboys.) I don't think he's necessarily wrong; I just don't remember it.

It would've been the right time for something like that to happen, though. *American Bandstand* with Dick Clark, syndicated out of Philadelphia, was drawing big ratings, and the local kids were also tuning in a local rock 'n' roll dance-party show on KOTV, Channel 6.

I do remember doing some Saturday afternoon shows down at the Cimarron, where I'd come in and set a record player up on a stand, and bring in people like Frances Self for interviews. There'd be an audience, but it wasn't anything big. And I remember running the board for Ray at KFMJ when he had Patsy Cline in for an interview on his weekend show. She was still recovering from a big car accident, so it would've had to have been not long after June 1961, when the crash happened.

What I do know for sure is that not too long after we met, Ray and I started thinking about ways to help boost my career, which wasn't exactly settin' the woods on fire at the time. I *was* starting to get a little name recognition with country-music people around the area, though, because of the simple fact that, unlike today, there just weren't very many places you could turn to on the radio dial and find country songs. If you were the deejay playing their kind of music, the real fans sought you out and knew your name. And a lot of times, you could parley that recognition into making records that might get up enough steam to get you a little notice nationally.

One of the guys who did that was named Marvin McCullough. He never had a giant hit, but he recorded several 45s in the early '60s, during the time he was working in Tulsa as a disc jockey for radio station KRMG, which broadcast out of the Cimarron Ballroom. He actually had a few singles released by Capitol, one of the biggest labels in the business, but the song of his I remember making the most noise, "Just for A Little While," came out on Boyd Records out of Oklahoma City. That was in 1961, and it was big enough that United Artists Records got involved and picked it up for national distribution.

Marvin was from Alabama. He'd landed in Tulsa around '57, after starting his radio career at a station in Fort Smith, Arkansas. When I joined KFMJ, he was the top country-music deejay in town.

Keep in mind that we're talking about the early '60s, when there weren't any full-time country stations. Even KFMJ had religious content in the mornings, you remember, before giving way to country in the afternoons. On KRMG, which broadcast all kinds of different programming, Marvin McCullough had—at one time—an early-morning show, a noon show, and a midnight show. In a story my collaborator Wooley did for the *Tulsa World*'s March 15, 1998, edition, McCullough's steel-guitarist Rocky Caple—who had a band I worked with a lot, Rocky Caple and the Shotguns—said, "People would come in as a studio audience and watch him when he was on the radio. The studio probably had seats for 40 people, but there was never enough room. People would be standing around against the walls. Even on his midnight show, he always had a studio full."

By the early '60s, neither Johnnie Lee Wills nor Leon McAuliffe were doing a lunchtime broadcast any more, and that helped Marvin's popularity a lot. In fact, one of his shows took over the noonday slot on KRMG that had belonged to Leon. So I'm sure he picked up a lot of the people who were accustomed to hearing Leon—or Johnnie Lee—during their lunches.

In addition to all those daily radio programs, Marvin also played out, fronting a band run by Gene Mooney, who had a Tulsa-based group for many years.

So Marvin McCullough was at the top of the Tulsa heap when it came to country music. Naturally, Ray and I spent a lot of our time and energy trying to figure out how to get me up to somewhere near that level.

One of the ways we went about it was to get me out on some dates with Frances Self and the Playmates, as well as some of the other Tulsa bandleaders like Ted Creekmore and Johnny Stills, a couple of guys I mentioned earlier. In those days, I didn't have my own band yet, and a lot of time I was still playing in places for the kitty, or sitting in with different groups around town. When Ray started booking me with Frances and the Playmates and the others, it helped me a lot. Whenever we were playing a dance or a show, I was able to plug our appearances on the air, so the people who listened to KFMJ would know where we were going to be and might be motivated to come out and see us. It was a good arrangement that worked for everyone, and I'm not saying that I started threatening Marvin McCullough's status as the king of the hill (although, looking back, he might have *thought* I was), but we did draw decent crowds and got a lot of work.

So I had a show, and I had a band. Now, the only thing McCullough had that I didn't was a record that would make a little noise for me nationally.

It's a funny thing, but Marvin himself ended up supplying it for me.

As I remember, the song had been pitched to him by Eddie Miller, the guy who'd co-written "Just for A Little While" and penned the flip side, "Maybe My Baby," on his own. Eddie was an Oklahoma boy, but he wasn't just a local guy trying to get local acts to record his songs. Remember "Release Me," that big hit for Ray Price and, later on, Englebert Humperdinck? That was one of Eddie's, and so was Carl Smith's "There She Goes." Working out of both the West Coast and Nashville at one time or another, he sold a whole bunch of songs to major country artists.

Marvin had recorded some of Eddie's other tunes besides "Just for A Little While" and "Maybe My Baby," so they must've had a pretty good relationship. But on one particular occasion Marvin was not too impressed by a number Eddie and another songwriter, Don Sessions, had pitched him. Marvin McCullough could be a pretty hard guy, and when the tune didn't do anything for him, he was just going to pitch the demo tape in the trash. Instead, for some reason, he passed it on to me. And when I gave it a listen I thought it was pretty doggone good.

So, one day in 1963 I went over to Oral Roberts' recording studio (remember, he owned KFMJ at this time). It was in the basement of a big building on Boulder Avenue that housed all his ministry operations. David Ingles came along as my piano player, and some members of Marvin's group, Rocky Caple & the Shotguns, were on the session—I'd been working with 'em quite a little bit myself. Rocky was there (not playing steel, as usual, but acoustic guitar), Vernon Walker played bass, and R.G. Mills picked the electric guitar. Melvin Bevenue was on drums, and the Vanguard Quartet, a group David Ingles had, came in to do background vocals. We cut the Eddie Miller-Don Sessions song that Marvin McCullough had rejected.

It was called "Thanks A Lot."

─ ★ ─

I don't know if I pointed this out before, but Ray Bingham and Leon McAuliffe were about as tight as you could get. Ray had started out as a fan of Leon and the Cimarron Boys, going to their shows and noon broadcasts, and it hadn't taken Leon long to see Ray's potential and love for the music. So he put Ray to work. At first, Ray was doing stuff like taking tickets and even sweeping up after shows. But by the time Ray and I became friends, he'd graduated to doing a lot of the booking for Leon at the Cimarron. (You remember, too, we had a little show on KFMJ that sometimes aired live from the ballroom.) So I'm sure it was the relationship between Leon and Ray that led to "Thanks A Lot" being released on Leon's own label, Cimarron Records. (The flip side, "Out of Your Heart," was written by yours truly). I think we may have even talked about it during one of those Saturday afternoon shows at the Cimarron.

Whatever the reasons, we got "Thanks A Lot" released on Leon's label. It may not have been Capitol or Decca, but it had a little bit of a national reach. And the record started taking off. If I'm remembering right, the first guy outside of Tulsa who started giving it some spins was Biff Collie, a pretty well-known deejay then, who worked at a big station called KFOX in Long Beach, California. Of course, the guys on KFMJ and I were playing it in the Tulsa market, and even some of the jocks over at the big rock 'n' roll station, KAKC, started putting it on their playlists. I especially remember two of the KAKC guys, Scooter Seagraves and Tom York, playing the fire out of it—so much that it actually got into what was called the KAKC Top 50 Survey. And it didn't just creep in for a week or two, either. I've got one of these weekly charts from March 25, 1963 that has "Thanks A Lot" at No. 4, right in between two records released by RCA—Skeeter Davis's "The End of the World" and Duane Eddy's "Boss Guitar." (No. 1 that week, in case you're wondering, was "Blame It on the Bossa Nova" by Eydie Gormé, on Columbia Records.) The rankings, according to a line at the bottom of the survey, were "based on sales, juke box plays and your requests to the new KAKC."

So I was getting some good airplay in town. Hell, Marvin McCullough even gave the single a spin on KRMG.

Yep, I said *a* spin. And that wasn't even legit, really. It was a 45 rpm record, of course, but when McCullough played it, he sped the turntable up to 78 rpm. That's the honest truth. Boy, was I mad. I think he did it because *he* was mad, or maybe a little bit jealous, since a song that he'd had the chance to record had started doing real good for someone else.

"Thanks A Lot" was doing so good, in fact, that Leon couldn't keep up with the demand for it. Because it was a surprise hit, he hadn't pressed enough copies to go around. And by the time he got back to the record plant to get some more copies made, another factor had been thrown in.

One of the biggest country-music acts in the world had taken notice of "Thanks A Lot," and he was impressed. So impressed, as a matter of fact, that he wanted to cut his own version.

I met Billy Parker at KFMJ radio in Tulsa, Oklahoma. Billy trained me for my radio shift in...one day. That was just the beginning of a whole host of experiences.

I consider Billy, an outstanding entertainer. He could always choose the best songs for the best flow of his radio show. He was careful to always think of the listener. Thank you, Billy,

THANKS—THANKS A LOT

for inspiring me with your creative jingles (ranging from automobile dealers to TV and appliance stores).

Many times Billy would go see a business owner...make a pitch to get him on the air, "clinching the deal" with a Billy Parker custom jingle (Billy and his guitar). As friends, our aim was to sell products and services and build goodwill for the client as well as promoting our station. I was thrilled when Billy's singing landed him a contract with a major recording label! His recordings were very popular, and they won him many fans.

From his childhood in Tuskegee, Oklahoma, to numerous awards and a Hall of Fame induction...WOW! I've always been proud to have Billy as my friend.

A Fan,

DAVID INGLES

CHAPTER SIX

At the time "Thanks A Lot" started taking off, I didn't really *know* Ernest Tubb. We'd met, and of course I'd played his records on my shows, but I couldn't say that we were buddies or anything like that. Most of the time I saw Ernest, he was on the stage and I was on the floor, watching him. The Cain's Ballroom was a regular stop for him and the Texas Troubadours on their tours, and I always tried to make his shows, because I loved the Troubadours' music.

Cal Smith was the Troubadours' front man then, and I had gotten to know Cal fairly well. He was an Oklahoma boy like me—born in the little town of Gans—and a fine singer who'd go on to have big hit records like "The Lord Knows I'm Drinking," "It's Time to Pay the Fiddler," and "Country Bumpkin." As I recall it, we first became acquainted at a place called the Uptown Club, on Tulsa's Main Street right down from the Cain's.

After Ernest's shows got finished, the band members would go back to the Downtowner Motel at Fourth Street and Cheyenne Avenue. That's where they always stayed. It wasn't very far from the Uptown Club, and Cal would come down and we'd set up there and have a jam session. Country music fans and pickers back then knew that the Uptown Club was the place to go after everything else closed down, so there were usually crowds to play for, but even if nobody was there but Cal and me, we were likely as not to pick and grin all night long—and I mean *all* night long. Several times, Ernest would send somebody down there or call the club and give Cal the message that they were leaving at nine o'clock, whether he showed up or not. So we'd have to hustle out to my car so I could drive him up to the Downtowner so he could get on the bus. Then I'd go home.

I'm sure it was Cal who gave his boss my number, which led to one of the more surprising things that happened to me back in those days, when "Thanks A Lot" was beginning to look more and more like a hit. One evening, the phone rang at home, and when I picked it up, a deep voice said, "Billy? This is Ernest Tubb."

I'd visited with Ernest a few times, nothing too serious, but I'd never talked to him over the phone. Still, I could tell it wasn't anyone prankin' me. Ernest had a very distinctive way of speaking; he sounded a lot like he did when he sang.

I'm sure I wondered why in the world Ernest Tubb was giving me a call at home. But I didn't have to wonder about it long. After a few pleasantries, he got down to business.

"Would it bother you, or do you think it would hurt your career," he asked me, "if I recorded 'Thanks A Lot'?"

All these years later, I don't remember exactly how I felt when he asked me that. I guess I was flattered, in a way, because he thought enough of my record to want to cover it himself. But I think I also knew somewhere in the back of my mind that if he cut it, his version would blow mine right out of the water. He was on Decca Records then, one of the biggest of the national labels, and they had plenty of firepower. Couple that with the Ernest Tubb name and there wasn't much doubt that Billy Parker's record of "Thanks a Lot" would be left in the dust.

(Because of the research John and Brett did, I know that my own version of "Thanks A Lot" was released on Decca, too—but only in England. I can't tell you how or why that happened, but I understand it also came out in Australia, on another label called W&G. This happened in '63, the same year Cimarron put it out in America.)

Of course, I didn't let Ernest know that I figured he was killing my chance to have a real radio hit. Instead, I said, "No. Certainly not. That'd be wonderful."

Well, it was wonderful, all right. Just not for me. Ernest covered it and it got all the way up to No. 3 on *Billboard* magazine's Country Singles chart. A couple of years later, Brenda Lee had a fair hit with it on the pop charts. And my own version died on the vine, just as I'd figured it would. I ended up not getting a dime from that record.

Let me take that back. Actually, I ended up making $500 off of it. That's the size of the check Don Sessions sent me many years ago, after Ernest's version hit. (You remember Don was the co-writer of "Thanks A Lot.") He said if I hadn't recorded it, Ernest would never have heard it, and he was grateful to me for being the one who got his song out there.

To this day, I wonder if Ernest called me because he thought I was the one who'd written "Thanks A Lot." I don't think, in all our years of knowing one another, I ever asked him. And I had plenty of chances, especially after joining his band.

But that wouldn't come for a few more years. In the time between, I had a couple of other places I had to go and things I had to do in the radio business as well as on TV. More important than that, I got married again, and this time it worked out better than I could've ever hoped.

Although Ernest's version of "Thanks A Lot" roared past my own recording of it, I kept cutting records during those days. One of the record-label connections I made back then, with a man named Russell Sims, became a part of my recording life for more than 30 years. Russell, who'd been associated with T. Texas Tyler back in the '50s, had started his Sims Records label out on the West Coast, but by the time I made his acquaintance, he'd moved to Nashville. The best I remember, we met each other because I'd started playing records by one of his artists, a rockabilly guy named Joe Poovey, on KFMJ.

The first Sims record I did was "The Line Between Love and Hate" b/w "I Hurt Me (Instead of You)," released in September of 1963. Both sides were written by Poovey, who was, like me, a disc jockey. He was associated with *The Big D Jamboree*, a show broadcast over

KRLD in Dallas, and recorded under a couple of different names. He had a pretty fair career in the business, but I don't think my versions of his tunes had much of anything to do with that.

It's kind of too bad, though, because "The Line Between Love and Hate" is a helluva song. If I ever had the chance, I'd record it again. But I don't know if it'd sell this time either, the way country music is now. It really lays the truth down in words, and I just don't think it would sell to today's audiences. It tells too much truth.

In July of 1964, Russell put out a second single on me: "Sounds Like A Winner," backed with a funny little tune called "Tatooed Lover." "Sounds Like A Winner" was written by Jean Chapel, a female songwriter who was a few years away from hitting it big with songs like Eddy Arnold's "Lonely Again" and Dean Martin's "Lay Some Happiness on Me," both released in 1967. "Sounds Like A Winner" had a good hook in its chorus—"Keep talkin', you sound like a winner to me"—but, sorry to say, Billy P.'s record on the Sims label did about as much for Jean Chapel as the first single had done for Joe Poovey.

A couple of years later, Russell Sims tried again with me. The A-side was called 'Hold My Hurt for Awhile," another Joe Poovey tune, and the flip was one called "Shut Your Big Fat Mouth," written by J.B. Davis and C. Davis—maybe a husband and wife team. Unfortunately, the third time wasn't the charm for me and Sims Records.

Still, these 45s began an association with Russell that lasted a long time and led to other recording projects.

The next year, 1965, 4-Star out of Los Angeles put out a single on me. The A-side was "Gold Rush Girl," written by Will Jones. The

B-side was called "If I Make It Through Tonight," and it was written by Gail Talley, who'd go on to have a nice career as a country-music songwriter, along with a young lady from Pennsylvania named Jeannie Seely, who had just started working for 4-Star at the time. I'm honored to have cut one of Jeannie's first songs, written well before she moved from the West Coast to Nashville and became a big star. I wish my single would've done more for her. But it didn't.

Earlier in this book, I told you about Pride Records, my own company, which I'll talk about more later. But I thought I ought to say something about another 45 I did, back in 1967. It was for BTR Records out of Tulsa, which only put out a handful of singles in both the rock 'n' roll and country fields—four of 'em by a country artist named Al Horn.

Even if you grew up in T-Town, you may not remember that label. But what if I told you that the "BTR" stood for Bill's T Records? And that Al Horn was not only the head of the BTR label, but also the owner of Bill's T Records, the biggest and best record store in Tulsa at the time? Lots of folks, country fans and rock 'n' rollers alike, remember that great old place over on Admiral and Harvard, which was full of 45s—including those that Horn himself did. I especially remember another of the country artists who had a record out on BTR, a big tall Indian boy named Dale Postoak. Mine was called "Baby I'm Gone" b/w "You Can Check on Me," and the A-side was written by a great Oklahoma entertainer, Carl Belew.

I can't recall the circumstances that led to me making that record, but Al Horn had a couple of his own records out around that time. I suspect the reason he recorded me was that he was looking for airplay on KFMJ, and I suspect he got it. But truthfully, if it was any good at all, I'd play *anyone's* record on my show. It's the same approach I took when I went to the all-night show on KVOO years later. I knew first-hand what the struggle was like for an artist to try and get *any* kind of airplay, and I liked to help people who were in the business, or trying to get in the business.

Through all the time I was in radio, I can honestly say that never changed.

~ ★ ~

By the time Pride Records came along, I'd already taken several trips down to Music City and back. Country was starting to make a little bit more noise nationally in those days, but it still wasn't anything like what it would start becoming in the '70s and '80s, so it was easier for a country music deejay to get recognized for what he was doing—not just locally, but nationally. My work as a disc jockey, in fact, was the reason for one of my trips, which I'll tell you about a little bit later.

In addition to holding down my shift at KFMJ, I was doing quite a bit of local TV. It was during this time I started picking up sponsors in Tulsa that would be with me for many years, beginning with Bradley Chevrolet and Horn Brothers Furniture. Horn Brothers Furniture, over on Third Street in Tulsa, was owned by a man who went by the name of Ike Horn. His real name was M.A. Eichorn, and he sponsored a show I was on called *The Longhorn Wingding*. It came on every Saturday at 6 p.m. over KTUL-TV, Channel 8. I remember having a whole lot of local acts on it, people like Johnny

Stills and Ted Creekmore. Later on, probably somewhere around 1970, it would become *The Horn Brothers Show*, but I was long gone by that time.

I also remember doing a regular show along the same lines for Ray Bradley Chevrolet in Broken Arrow. Truthfully, about the only thing I really recall is the theme song I used to sing, which went to the tune of that old song, "It's A Long Way to Tipperary." I'd sing, "It's not a long way to Broken Arrow/It's not a long way to go/To Bradley Chevrolet."

Funny what you remember, isn't it?

It was like *The Longhorn Wingding*, with lots of guests coming in to do songs. Most all of them were different entertainers from around Tulsa. One of the biggest names I had on the show was Carl Belew, from Salina, Oklahoma—about fifty miles east of Tulsa. By the early 1960s he was pretty well established as a country artist, with Top 10 hits like "Am I That Easy to Forget" and "Hello Out There." I suspect I got him while he was back home visiting.

Those were the great days of live local television, and it seems to me like I was doing one TV show after another for years. And while they all kind of blend into one another now, some 60 years or so down the road, I can truthfully say I enjoyed the heck out of every one of 'em.

It was while all this was going on that the folks who ran KFMJ decided to send me up to KFDI in Wichita. The brother-in-law of Ron Blue, who'd first hired me, was at KFDI then, so I know *how it*

was that I got transferred to KFDI—I just can't remember exactly *why* management asked me to change locations. I do know that it was a bigger station, so that could've had something to do with it. I may have looked at it as a step up the radio ladder.

You might recall that Frank and Mike Lynch had bought KFDI after they sold KFMJ to Oral Roberts in 1963. Maybe the Lynches being there was a factor in my going there as well, but I'm not sure about that. When I get to thinking about KFDI, I *do* remember something that I guess is pretty trivial, but interesting: I understand that at one time it had been called KFBI, but the Feds came in and made 'em change it so no one would think it was connected with the Federal Bureau of Investigation.

Although KFDI was a bigger outfit, moving there didn't come without some challenges. It came at a time, like I said earlier, when I'd started doing a pretty good amount of local TV. It took about four hours to get to Wichita from Tulsa, and for a while there, I was burning up the road going back and forth to meet my different broadcast obligations. Finally, I moved my stuff to Wichita and started living in a back room right there at the station.

I can't tell you how long I was on the air at KFDI. It wasn't too long, but I do remember that I was there when I got my first national award.

The hub of country-music broadcasting was Nashville's big radio station WSM, and Grant Turner wasn't just the voice of the *Grand Ole Opry*, which ran on WSM, but also the voice of the station itself. He had a program called *Mr. DJ USA* that recognized disc jockeys from all over America, and in the early '60s, I got the call to go down and be on that show—which I was happy to do. I knew it might help my name recognition with the folks who ran the labels in Nashville, and I knew the publicity sure wouldn't hurt KFDI.

Just about all I remember about being on *Mr. DJ USA* was that whoever was supposed to give me the Mr. DJ USA plaque, or trophy, or whatever it was, didn't make it to the show, and Carl and Pearl Butler, the husband and wife who'd had such a big hit with "Don't Let Me Cross Over," presented it to me instead. I remember them interviewing me and talking about the business with me over the air. That was quite a thrill. Back then, most of the country-music people were very down-to-earth, but there was still royalty like the Butlers. Grant Turner and WSM carried a lot of weight in the industry, too.

After KFDI, but before I went back to Tulsa and KFMJ, I spent a few months doing a daily show at a third station, KLPR in Oklahoma City, which was owned by a friend of mine named Jack Beasley. After all these years, I've forgotten why I took that particular job. I know he didn't have anything to do with KFMJ or KFDI; fact of the matter is, his Big Chief Broadcasting Company owned KTOW in Sand Springs, and he meant for it to be a rival to KFMJ. Jack had been in a group called the Chuck Wagon Boys, who had a TV show on WKY in Oklahoma City, before becoming a radio-station owner. He had a lot of connections in the business.

I remember being friends with Jack before he hired me, and when I did go to Oklahoma City and KLPR (which I used to say stood for "Keep Listening to Pretty Records"), it was to do the morning show, which even then most deejays thought was the best and most important shift to have. Maybe that's one of the reasons I relocated.

Again, I wasn't there long. Ray Bingham remembers coming through OKC with Leon McAuliffe in 1965 and sitting in on the show with me, so that gives us a little bit of a time frame. And I was there long enough to move into a house, at least for a while, that was close to the radio station. While I was in town, I also did a little work for Jack's Oklahoma City TV station, which was also called KLPR. I recall doing a weekly show that a lot of people still seem to remember for the Mathis brothers and their furniture store.

Jack drank a little, so he could be kind of erratic from time to time. I recall once, when I was doing my morning show, he came in and took me off the air so I could drive with him to Shawnee to visit some of his friends. That didn't seem too professional to me. In fact, him pulling me off the air like that may have started me thinking about going back to Tulsa.

The day I left OKC for good, I remember filling up with gas at a self-service station there and being so excited about getting back to Tulsa that I drove off with the hose still attached to my car. I suspect that by that time I was plenty ready to leave Oklahoma City and KLPR, morning show or no morning show.

Back in Tulsa, I kept on doing what I'd been doing—playing records at KFMJ, doing local television shows, and recording whenever I could, along with playing dances and shows. Pride Records was up and running, too, so I was pretty busy.

THANKS—THANKS A LOT

I know this was when I started playing a lot with Rocky Caple and the Shotguns, which more or less became my band. A couple of the guys in it, Caple and Vernon Walker, had been on the "Thanks A Lot" session at Oral Roberts' studio. I also had a guy who would become one of my best friends, Roy Ferguson, on guitar, Melvin Bevenue on the drums, and Roy's wife, Candy Noe, singing with me.

We started playing quite a few different dances and events, including the Johnnie Lee Wills Tulsa Stampede, a big rodeo that Johnnie Lee and Bob Wills's business manager, O.W. Mayo, had started with Bob back in the 1930s. If you look at the Official Souvenir Program for the 28th annual Tulsa Stampede, which took place May 3-8, 1966, you'll see an ad for a Saturday night rodeo dance at the Cain's Ballroom with "Music by Johnnie Lee Wills with Billy Parker and His Western Band." My group would also set up in the stands at the rodeo arena, where a little stage had been set up, and play for the folks between events.

It was there, somewhere between May 3 and May 8 in 1966, that I met Jerri Hamblin. Six weeks later, we were married.

Fifty-five years later, and counting, we still are.

Looking back on it, I know that being the wife of a musician and disc jockey wasn't easy—especially when that musician and deejay was named Billy Parker—but Jerri hung in there and supported me as I chased my dreams. From the very beginning, she has been my inspiration, and a lot of the songs I've recorded I've sung with her in mind, especially "Lord, If I Make It to Heaven (Can I Bring My Own Angel Along)," one of the first of my singles to make the national charts. I think that song and the way I sing it tells you a lot about how I've always felt toward Jerri.

⭒

I kept plugging along, playing records over KFMJ, making personal appearances and recording. I had a kind of breakthrough in that last department the year after I married Jerri, when I landed on Decca Records for a single called "I'm Drinking All the Time." It would be the first of five I'd do for that big-time label, and I had a big-time producer, too: Owen Bradley, who was even then a legend in the business. I always tell people that I went to Nashville to do records with Owen Bradley and I've been owin' Bradley ever since. The truth is, those records were really the only ones I ever made any money on. They didn't make much of a noise nationally, although they did get played some, but because it was a musicians'-union deal they had to pay you. I can't remember exactly how much the checks were for, but I think I made a few hundred dollars. Before I cashed 'em, I made copies and had them framed. I've still got 'em around somewhere.

Looking back, I know that Ernest did an awful lot to connect me with Decca, which was the label that put out his records as well. And even though Cal Smith was recording for Kapp at the time I got my deal, I feel sure he had plenty to do with it as well. I think you could also give an assist to Jack Greene, who, like Ernest, was on Decca. I guess I'll never know exactly how it worked, but I believe Jack and Cal, both of whom spent a good amount of time as Texas Troubadours, brought my name up to E.T., maybe convinced

THANKS—THANKS A LOT

him that I had a little bit of talent, and Ernest then went to Owen Bradley and Decca and got me a recording contract. I know that in addition to being E.T.'s producer, Bradley played piano on a lot of his Nashville recording sessions. They knew each other very well. I suspect Owen Bradley would've taken Ernest's advice on recording someone like me.

Some folks have naturally figured that Ernest got me my Decca deal as a payback for my saying I was okay with him recording "Thanks A Lot." I've even thought about that myself. But even if there's some truth to that, I'm sure that wasn't the whole story. He didn't need my permission to make his own version of "Thanks," and he didn't need to feel bad about having the hit on it instead of me. I think he promoted me to Owen Bradley and Decca because he was a gentleman, known for helping people in the business—Cal Smith, Jack Greene, Stonewall Jackson, and many, many more. He was just a perfect person, really, and all my dealings with him, my faith in him, and his faith in me, just came natural, I think. It wasn't phony. He didn't owe me anything and I didn't owe him anything, except to do the best job I could do when I went to work for him as a Texas Troubadour—and when I went into the studio to record the sessions he'd set up for me.

As things turned out, most of those Decca 45s of mine were released while I was working for E.T. as the front man for his Texas Troubadours.

But I'm getting ahead of myself.

I continued to play around Tulsa in '66 and '67, and one of the places my band and I worked a lot was the Cain's Ballroom. Ernest and the Troubadours played there regularly, too. For years and years, it was one of their stops when they were out on the road. In December of '61, they even recorded a live disc for Decca at the old ballroom. If you look at the cover of the album, which was called *On Tour*, they're all posing at the Cain's, and on the back it says the album was recorded at "the famous Cain's Ballroom in Tulsa, Oklahoma." To be truthful, though, it was actually cut in a Nashville studio, with crowd noises added later on. From what I understand, the folks at the Cain's just made too much noise for the engineers to get a decent recording. That's the Cain's Ballroom for you!

At that time, Bob Wills was long gone from Tulsa, and while his brother Johnnie Lee was still in town, he was busy running a very successful western-wear store with his wife, Irene, and his son, John Thomas, and he wasn't playing a whole lot at the Cain's or anywhere else. A man named Alvin Perry, along with his wife, Ada, ran the ballroom then after having worked many years there for O.W. Mayo.

Alvin, truth to tell, could be a little bit of a hard-ass. Once, back in the early '60s, he'd actually had Ray Bingham and me thrown out of the place. That was when the competition was fierce between the Cain's and Leon McAuliffe's Cimarron Ballroom, and because Ray worked for Leon, Alvin thought we were spying on his operation one night when we came over to watch an act—I think it was Buck Owens—and had us removed from the premises. (The bouncer who hauled us out the door was the brother of our friend Gene Crownover, who played steel guitar for Bob Wills a lot in Bob's later years.) As we were being escorted out, Alvin Perry was standing by the door, telling us we'd never set foot in the Cain's again.

Of course, things change, and I never had any trouble with Alvin when I was performing there. I remember one particular night in 1967, when I was on the stage with the band. Whoever was in the Cain's office at the time got a call and came down to tell me that Jerri had been rushed to St. Francis Hospital. I don't remember whether I had my guitar on or not at the time, but as soon as I heard the news I jumped off the stage. I thought I'd broken my dadgum leg; cowboy boots weren't the best thing to be jumping around in. But I kept going, and I remember hopping over the white picket fence they had set up in front of the stage and taking off for the front door, headed for St. Francis.

A little later, our first boy, Billy Joe Parker, was born.

Cal Smith did a lot for me, and I'm just about sure he was the person who recommended me to Ernest when a vacancy was coming up in the Texas Troubadours. Now that I think about it, Cal was the one who first called me about it. He wanted to know if I was interested in taking over for him as Ernest's front man. Cal already had two or three solo albums out on Kapp by then, and while he hadn't had any huge hits yet—those would come later—he was making the national charts with both his albums and singles. And he wanted to follow in the footsteps of Jack Greene, the Jolly Green Giant, who'd left his job as the Texas Troubadours' drummer and singer a year or two earlier—with Ernest's encouragement—to take a shot at a solo career. Of course, that worked out great.

If I'm not mistaken, E.T. and the band were on the road, and Cal phoned me from a restaurant in Sallisaw, Oklahoma, where they'd stopped to eat. Basically, what he asked me was, "Billy, how would you like to be a Texas Troubadour?"

I didn't know what to say. I couldn't find any words. I remember thinking, "Good Lord! Why *me*?"

I did really want to take another step up in the business, and being the guy who introduced a country-music legend at all of his shows and got to do a couple of songs with his band—which was full of great musicians—sure seemed to be another rung on the ladder. On the other hand, I didn't particularly want to make any sort of big move. If I took the job, I'd have to move to Nashville; I couldn't do it from Tulsa. And Jerri and I had built a pretty good life for ourselves. We had a nice home. We had a son who was still a baby. Once I said yes, all three of us would all be uprooted and headed into the unknown.

So I told Cal, honestly and truthfully, "Of *course*, I'd love it. And thank you. But you know what, hoss? I've got to speak to the wife about this."

He said he understood, and told me where I could get hold of them over the next few days, after Jerri and I had talked. So I went home, and we went over it. It wasn't a hard sell. She knew me.

"Yes," she said. "We ought to do that. You've worked hard all these years, and you want to be in the business. This is your chance to do it, and I'm with you."

I won't kid you. Even though I had Jerri's blessing, I was very nervous about making that great change in my life. And when I talked to Ernest himself, after a couple of days, he didn't do much to calm me down. "It's a tough old road, son," he told me. "We're working a lot. It ain't easy being out there all the time, riding the bus everywhere, staying on the go. You have to be able to take it." Looking back, I know he wanted to make sure I knew, best I could, what I was in for, and he kept stressing how hard he and the band were working.

He wasn't kidding, either. They weren't just working Friday and Saturday nights, or Saturdays and Sundays, like a lot of the acts do today. They were playing somewhere just about every dad-gum day of the week, maybe getting a Monday off every once in a while, but basically never less than five nights out of seven. They were gone all the time. The way things were in his private life then, he didn't want to stay home. Get him $600 on Monday and $700 on Tuesday and let's go.

I talked to him for a while, and then I let him know I'd take the job. After I got off the phone, I told Jerri about the conversation, but I didn't tell her everything, especially about how much he'd talked about the road life. I'd made the commitment, and not long after that, we found a place in Hendersonville, Tennessee, about 20 miles northeast of Nashville, where a lot of people in the country-music business had homes.

It was both a sad time and a happy time in our lives. Just after we made the decision to leave town and join Ernest, my dad passed away. At age 75, a stroke killed him, and we stayed in town for our grieving and for the funeral service. My dad had always loved country music, and he was glad that I loved it, too. But he was gone before I ever had any songs on the charts or got any awards for being a country disc jockey (except for that *Mr. DJ USA* thing from WSM). I've always regretted that he didn't live to see me doing a little bit better in the business.

When we left Tulsa, we had heavy hearts. From the time the moving van pulled up in front of our house, until we got settled in Hendersonville, it was a tough time. I won't lie. I had my doubts about what I was doing—making a move far from home with a wife and a baby and then having to jump on a bus and hit the road, which is exactly what I was getting ready to do.

So there were sad and anxious parts to it. On the other hand, I was excited to be working for Ernest Tubb, a real country star—who also turned out to be one of the greatest men I've ever known.

> *Billy Parker was not only a great entertainer and recording artist during his career, he was a major force of promotion in that area for all of us who were making records. His door was always open and he gave as much time to a new artist as he did the established stars of the day. I appreciate not only his support of my career but I treasure his personal friendship as well.*
> ~ **Jeannie Seely** ~

These weren't from the first time I played the *Midnite Jamboree* with Ernest and the Texas Troubadours, but you can get an idea of the size of the "stage" in the downtown Nashville Record Shop location where we broadcast live on Saturday nights.

CHAPTER SEVEN

The first time I sang as a member of the Texas Troubadours was on the *Midnite Jamboree*, a radio show broadcast live from the Ernest Tubb Record Shop in Nashville. It was a Saturday night show, and as you can tell from the title, it came on the air at midnight over WSM (and still does).

I should say it was *supposed* to start at midnight. But it followed WSM's *Grand Ole Opry,* and on the night I made my debut as a Texas Troubadour, Marty Robbins was starring on the *Opry*. When he was in the driver's seat, the show *never* got finished by midnight, because he'd sing a song and when he finished he'd wave at the crowd to keep 'em cheering. It was intentional. He'd egg 'em on. Of course, he'd get an encore anyway with the *Opry* crowd, but he would *over*-encore. Of all the acts to play the *Opry*, he's the only one I ever remember who held us up like that. And he *enjoyed* it. Ernest loved Marty, but it always aggravated him that Marty would cause his own show to come on late. Sometimes it could be as much as an hour.

I don't think I had to wait quite that long to make my *Midnite Jamboree* debut—but it felt like years. If you're thinking I would've been plenty nervous even without the wait, you're absolutely right.

By that time, Cal Smith was no longer a Texas Troubadour, although he'd later on ride in the bus with us for a couple of shows every once in awhile. But he never trained me to be his replacement or gave me any real idea of what to expect. We didn't have any overlap. And there weren't any rehearsals or anything else. I just showed up for work and got put on the air and into the homes of thousands and thousands of listeners.

Of course, by this time I knew my way around a radio microphone. But I was still intimidated. This was a different level, bigger than KFMJ or even KFDI. E.T., the way I saw him, was a Hollywood star, and I was nervous because I thought, "Hell. I can't satisfy him. I'm not going to fit in." I really didn't feel like I should be a part of this band, with all these great musicians. I wasn't good enough to belong with Steve Chapman, E.T.'s guitarist at the time, with Wayne Jernigan on drums, or Buddy Charleton on steel guitar. Why had I even done this? I couldn't play with these guys. I even played guitar out of meter. (So did Ernest, but that's another story. Truth is, he'd play one meter, I'd play another, and we'd make the rest of the band members mad.)

Those were the kinds of thoughts going through my mind while I waited for Marty Robbins to take his final damn curtain call so we could get started. Before I even sang a note with Ernest and the

Troubadours, I was ready to get back to Tulsa and familiar surroundings, or at least back to 163 Roberta Drive in Hendersonville, where we were living, and say to Jerri, "Let's go home."

But that wasn't going to happen. At least, not on *that* night. So when the voice of Grant Turner brought us on, there I was on that dinky stage at the Ernest Tubb Record Shop, singing and playing guitar. With my cowboy hat on—Ernest insisted that all of us guys in the band wear hats—I looked like I was about three feet tall.

After all these years, I'm not sure what my first song was as the new front man for the Texas Troubadours. It wasn't "Thanks A Lot"—I'll tell you *that*. I think it may have been "My Window Faces the South," that old western-swing tune that Bob Wills and lots of others had done. Or maybe it was "San Antonio Rose." I know it was something that the band knew and could jam on.

What I *do* remember, like it was yesterday, was my legs shaking so hard I didn't know if I could walk—or even talk, for that matter. Luckily, I didn't have to do any emceeing that first night. We just took off after Grant Turner's intro.

There were six of us in the Troubadours, on that little-bitty postage-stamp-sized stage in Ernest's store down on 417 Broadway. When the whole band got up there, we'd barely fit. I remember a good crowd being there that first time I played, most of 'em watching us, some of 'em roaming around and buying albums and stuff.

Right after that, we jumped on Ernest's bus, the Green Hornet, and took off for Eau Claire, Wisconsin. And just like that, I started my career as a member of one of country music's best-known—and hardest-working—traveling bands.

THANKS—THANKS A LOT

The distance between Nashville and Eau Claire is right around 800 miles. (I looked it up.) In the Green Hornet, that amounted to about 12-15 hours on the road, not counting stops. And for every one of those 800 miles, my knees were knocking so hard I thought I was going to break some bones in my legs. As I found out later, sometimes people who were playing on the same bill with us would hitch a ride on E.T's bus, and that first time we headed out to Eau Claire, Jeannie Seely came along with us—the same Jeannie Seely who'd written the flip side of the 4-Star record I'd cut a few years earlier. She'd gone so far so fast that a year earlier she'd been awarded a Grammy for Best Female Country Vocal for her first big hit, "Don't Touch Me." Just as she did later on, when she was touring and singing with Jack Greene, she encouraged me a lot. I remember her talking to me on the way to Wisconsin, telling me stuff like, "Now, Billy, you can do this. You know you can do it." I'm sure she knew how nervous I was, because I've never been much good at hiding it.

So even with Jeannie in my corner, I sweated and shook all the way to Eau Claire, where we were playing an afternoon show at some sort of auditorium. My job was to come out, do three songs with the band, and then bring Ernest onto the stage. We had a big show. Jeannie was on the concert, and Bobby and Sonny, the Osborne Brothers, doing their bluegrass music. It seems like Bobby Lewis was on the bill, too. Later on, he became a good friend of mine. We still keep in touch. At the time, he had country hits like "How Long Has It Been" and "Love Me and Make It All Better," but I guess the thing that made him stand out most from the rest of the pack was the instrument he played. It was a six-string guitar-lute, which you didn't see much in country music then (and still don't).

I didn't have to introduce any of those great performers. All I had to do was warm up the crowd with my three songs, give Ernest his intro, and then step back and play with the rest of the band. As hard as I've tried, I can't remember which songs I did before I brought Ernest on, but I keep thinking one of them was "T-U-L-S-A, Straight Ahead," which Leon McAuliffe had recorded many years before, when he had his Cimarron Ballroom in Tulsa. The band knew it, and knew how to play it, so we did it. We hadn't had time to do a lot of rehearsing.

It all kind of went by in a blur, and before I knew it, I was saying, "Now, ladies and gentlemen, please welcome the Texas Troubadour, Ernest Tubb!" I didn't have any trouble with that part of it at all, because I'd done so much radio. Up came E.T., and I stepped back and just played rhythm guitar the rest of the night. I was still out of meter, and I know I sounded terrible, but it was okay because my guitar wasn't amplified.

So there I stood, strumming along behind my new boss, the big country-music star Ernest Tubb. I was still nervous and shaky, but as I continued to play and watch Ernest and the crowd, another emotion came into play. I guess you could call it a sense of pride. It's hard to explain, exactly, but after all those times of watching Ernest and the Troubadours play on the stage of the Cain's Ballroom—of watching him from the fan side of things—I had suddenly crossed over. Now, I was looking out at the fans, who were watching *me*.

I guess the best way to put it is this way: At that moment, I felt like a champion.

THANKS—THANKS A LOT

Although I never told Jerri how I was feeling, it took me a number of trips to get over my nervousness about being a Texas Troubadour and to shake the feeling of wanting to leave and go back home. Fortunately, that band was on the road right away, so it was maybe only a week or two before I'd calmed down enough to start enjoying it. I also began to think about my future. Decca was still going to put out some more 45s with me, and I figured, "Well, if I can get this recording thing going, I can do like Cal's doing now. I can hit the road and make my own mind up about where I want to work, and who I want to work with, all of that." Don't get me wrong. I took a lot of pride in working with Ernest, but from the very beginning I realized that what he told me to expect when I first talked to him about being a Troubadour was absolutely right: He worked *all* the time. It wore you out.

As I remember, Ernest paid me $35 a night, and I think the rest of the band was about the same. Now, this is 1968 through some of 1970, so that was more money then than it is now. Still, it's really not a hell of a lot—plus, the nights we didn't work, we didn't get paid. Of course, we were pretty much working every night, so that wasn't too much of an issue. If we weren't on the road on a Saturday, for instance, we'd go to Ernest's record store and play the *Midnite Jamboree*. Sometimes, we'd do the *Grand Ole Opry* itself. If you were a member of the *Opry*, like Ernest was, you had to do so many *Opry* shows a year, so I ended up on that famous stage quite a little bit.

I'll never forget my *Grand Ole Opry* debut. The Texas Troubadours' front man always got to sing one song before bringing E.T. on, so I knew I was going to be in the spotlight. Looking back on it, I know I had to be awful nervous, but I imagine I also had a good feeling about finally appearing on the show my dad and I had listened to together for years, standing at the microphone just liked I'd dreamed of doing as a kid. I had some pride in knowing I'd gotten that far. But in addition to the pride *I* felt, there was another Pride involved, too—the great country star Charley Pride. I had to follow him, which was a little like a kid just up from the minors following Hank Aaron to the plate in a major-league baseball game. (Now that I think about it, Charley almost made it as a baseball player himself.)

Now, at this time, Charley was starting to really take off. As an RCA Victor artist, he'd already had country hits like "Just Between You and Me" and "Does My Ring Hurt Your Finger." But in those days, there wasn't all this access to information about artists that we have now. I know he'd been on the *Opry* at least once before that night, but there were still a lot of people out there—and in the audience at the Ryman Auditorium—who'd never actually seen him, or even a photo of him, before. I can't remember the song I did when I followed him onstage; what I *do* remember is waiting in the wings and hearing a big gasp from the audience when he came out. They just couldn't believe he was a black man.

Being the front man for the Texas Troubadours *was* a big step up for me in my career. Sure, I'd met lots of national country performers as a deejay back in Tulsa, or opening for 'em with my band. But now, I'd hooked up with one of the biggest stars in the business, and I was treated more or less as an equal by E.T.'s contemporaries.

Take Jack Greene, for instance. As I mentioned earlier, he'd been with the Texas Troubadours before going out on his own. We worked a lot of shows with him and his Jolly Green Giants. (For those who don't remember, Jack was a tall guy with a deep voice, and his Jolly Green Giant nickname came from the famous cartoon figure that advertised, and still does, frozen and canned vegetables.) Jeannie Seely was touring with him and the band at the time, and they made a great pair. They were another act recorded by Owen Bradley.

Both Jack and Jeannie were always good to me, always encouraging. I learned a lot from watching and listening to them on stage—they had a certain "feel" with a song that I tried to pick up for myself. They knew how to express the words in a song, how to put that feel into it. Just listen to Jack sing "There Goes My Everything." That's the kind of thing I learned from listening to him.

I first worked with Jim Ed Brown when E.T. did a New York tour. He was a terrific entertainer, too, and he became a great mentor for me. We'd talk a lot about the business. He knew the business. Jim Ed and the Browns, his sisters, had been in the business so many years and had recorded a bunch. He gave me good advice, and he never failed to give me encouragement—even later, when I was at KVOO and he'd come through to do a casino show or something and I'd emcee it. He's one of the nicest guys I've ever met in my life.

Of course, Dolly Parton is one of the great entertainers. But she was pretty good at changing diapers, too. One night when I was playing the *Midnite Jamboree* at Ernest's record shop, Dolly picked up Billy Joe and changed his diaper, right there backstage. I tried to get her to change mine, but she wouldn't do it.

I remember Dolly as being happy and jovial. She was with Porter Wagoner then, and she'd sometimes ride the bus with us. Ernest would get off the Green Hornet and get in Porter's bus so they could play poker together, and Dolly would ride with us.

By the time I got with Ernest, Bob Wills had sold off the Texas Playboys name and was touring as a solo act along with his singer, guitar player, and right-hand man, Tag Lambert. He and Tag would appear with other bands behind them; when you hear the old musicians say that they played with Bob Wills—and I've heard it hundreds of times—what it means a lot of times is that they were in one of the house bands Bob appeared with in those days. So, if you want to put it that way, I played with Bob Wills, too. (Of course, I worked with his brother—my great friend Johnnie Lee Wills— both before and after I joined up with E.T.)

In the late '60s, the promoter Hap Peebles put together a tour of maybe four or five dates through Oklahoma, Kansas, and Missouri. Bob and Tag were on the show with us, and the Texas Troubadours backed them. So I can truthfully say that I played rhythm guitar behind Bob Wills. I even had the opportunity to visit with him some. It was after he'd had his first stroke, and you could tell—he had a lisp from it and couldn't talk just right. I've got a picture of him and me backstage. He was nice, and he loved Ernest. Ernest loved him. They were the story. Not me. But I got to be a part of that story.

Getting to be a part of Ernest Tubb's story, in fact, was a great blessing in my life.

Previous to my joining him, E.T. had been into the bottle pretty bad, smoking those cigarettes and drinking. He wasn't ashamed of it. He wished he hadn't, but he wasn't ashamed. He'd talk to me about it on the bus. "Son," he'd say, "you shouldn't drink and you shouldn't smoke." And the guys in the band that smoked—like I did, at the time—would hide from him when we lit up.

His best friend ever was Red Foley, who had his own problems with alcohol. And Ernest had been a very good friend of Hank Williams and knew what Hank Williams had been through with the drinking and all that stuff. So he didn't lecture me, but he'd say, `Son, that's not the life to have in this business." He knew those guys and he himself had already been there and done that. He had a rule for all of the band: no drinking before a show and, I think, for two hours afterwards. Maybe he didn't want people to see us having a drink after the show; more likely, he just didn't want to see it himself.

Ernest Tubb taught me a lot of things. Maybe the biggest was to be patient. Lots of times when we were on the road, he'd sit up front for a while before he went to bed, and we'd have little visits. I'd sit there with him in that old Green Hornet, and with James Price, who was the driver, and we'd talk. He'd talk a lot about the business, and about his great pal Red Foley. Like I said, from listening to him, I learned to be patient, and also not to be disappointed if I didn't make it big in the business. He'd helped so many people—like me—and seen so much with people over the years. As far as I was concerned, he knew the business better than anyone else. He knew the business, respected the business, and respected the *people* in the business.

I don't believe I ever saw E.T. get mad, or even real aggravated. But that doesn't mean that he couldn't lay down the law. And believe me, I'm speaking with the voice of experience.

BILLY PARKER

Billy's a very special person in country music. He always has been. He's not only a great artist but he's done so much for all the other artists by playing their music, supporting their music, and pushing their music when he was in a position to really help them. He's one of a kind. He's just a special, special guy. I worked with him on the road when he was with Ernest Tubb but more than that he's remained a friend. And he's been a friend to country music ever since I first met him.

~ **BOBBY LEWIS** ~

Ernest Tubb, Jim Ed Brown, Bobby Lewis, and me.
One of my first tours with the Texas Troubadours in 1968.

Me and the boss man, Ernest Tubb, in 1968.

CHAPTER EIGHT

I think we were somewhere in the Carolinas when I finally decided to do it. We'd played at a fairgrounds somewhere and it had just rained and stormed something fierce the whole time we were playing. They'd put up something to make a kind of roof over us, but the weather was so bad there wasn't but about 50 or 75 people brave enough to be out there in the stands listening to us. Of course, we still did our whole show. Even if there'd only been two of 'em out there, Ernest would not let the people down.

Afterwards, it was still raining when we packed up and left town in the bus. It had been a rough night—one of those times I thought, "What am I doing here?" But for some reason, I thought it would be a good opportunity to talk to E.T. about the thing that had been bugging me.

For quite a while, I'd been griping to the guys—not to Ernest—about having to wear a cowboy hat when we were on stage. In all the time previous to my becoming a Texas Troubadour, I'd *never* worn a hat, and I didn't like doing it now. I could come up with lots of reasons why: I'd sweat inside the hat, it made me look like I was about two feet tall, things like that. The guys—Buddy Charleton, Steve Chapman, all of 'em—agreed with me that it was b.s. and that someone ought to say something to E.T. about it. Of course, I was the one they kind of nominated to do the job. Looking back, I guess it was always right, since I was the one doing the biggest part of the bitching.

By that time, I'd been with Ernest maybe six or eight months—enough time to feel brave enough to do that. So that night, in the middle of a rainstorm, leaving what had been a terrible gig, I made my move.

I remember a lot of what happened next real well. Ernest was in the back of the Green Hornet, where he had a little curtain you could pull shut. Behind that was where he had his little wooden icebox full of Coca-Cola in bottles, and his cases of Beanee Weenees. I think he had some cans of Wolf Brand Chili back there, too. He loved chili. But I know he kept boxes full of those Beanee Weenees. He ate 'em all the time, washing them down with Coca-Cola.

When I headed back to see E.T., we were still on the way out of town, the rain splashing all around us, and I remember feeling the bus go over some railroad tracks, real slow. The rest of the guys in the band were up in the front of the bus. I was doing this job by myself.

I didn't really want them to hear what I was saying to Ernest, so I went back where he was and pulled that curtain shut—like the band members couldn't hear me through a curtain!—and Ernest was there eating his Beanee Weenees and drinking his Coca-Cola.

I cleared my throat and said, "Ernest, I've been thinking. I have these doggone headaches and my hair's messed up all the time"—I forget exactly what I said, but I was making up excuses—"and one thing I'd like to do if I could is quit wearing a hat on stage. It really bothers me. It's always bothered me to wear a hat." I went on and on and on.

When I stopped to take a breath—and I remember this as if it were today—he said, "Son, no, you don't have to wear that hat. But you don't have to be a Texas Troubadour, either."

I don't remember what I said after that. I may have even thanked him. But I know I pulled that curtain and got my ass back up to the front of the bus—where the rest of the guys were all giggling and snickering and punching each other. They'd eavesdropped, of course, and they thought what I'd said and what Ernest had said back was all real hilarious.

I never asked Ernest for any special favor like that again. And I kept wearing the hats, one green, one purple, and one red, to go along with the suits we wore.

Now that I look back on it, I think maybe Ernest got as big a kick out of my request as the rest of the band. In fact, someone might have tipped him that I was going to come in that night and try to get him to let me stop wearing a hat.

Like I said earlier, we traveled a whole lot, and one of my jobs was to check us into hotels when we were on the road. We'd sleep on the bus, but once we got to where we were playing, we'd stay in a hotel. In Houston, for instance, we'd stay at the Texas State Hotel and then work the surrounding areas for four or five days, using the hotel as our base. Then, after we'd worked all our jobs in that area, we'd go on to California or back East or wherever we were booked. A lot of times, we'd be out on the road for at least a couple of weeks straight.

For Ernest, family came first. Sometimes, one or two of his kids would ride the bus with us on a short tour, and Ernest made sure his wife, Olene, was always taken care of. We'd get ready to go on the road, and Olene would stack the bus up with boxes of albums. I think there were 25 to a box—these were the old big vinyl LPs, not CDs—and the boxes would be stacked so high in so many places that you could hardly get to your bunk. She'd really stuff the bus, because, as I understood it, the money from selling those records went to her, even though she didn't go on the road with us. James Price, the bus driver, sold the records at our shows. Wherever we were playing, he'd set them up by the stage, and after the show we'd all go down there and sign them for people. Even if it took five hours, E.T. would make sure every album that got bought was autographed. It was good to sell as many as we could as quick as we could, so there'd be more room to move around in the bus. The best scenario would've been to sell 'em all on our first day out, but there were far too many for us to do that.

Ernest, like I said earlier, was really easy to work for. He was mostly businesslike, I'll say that, but didn't have any kind of "star" attitude. I don't remember him being smart-alecky to anybody, or crude, or actively unfriendly. Still, there was one situation where you didn't want to bother E.T. with anything, and that was during breakfast when we were staying at a hotel.

Usually at breakfast, the guys in the band—those of us who could make it—would all sit together and talk and maybe cut up a little. But E.T. would come in and take a seat by himself with his newspaper. He'd spend his whole mealtime reading the newspaper. If someone came up and asked him for an autograph, he'd oblige them, but that was pretty much the time that he wanted to be totally alone with his paper.

We didn't have a road manager. But there was always somebody who had to check everyone in to the hotel and tell the band members where to go and when to get there—and chew them out if they didn't make it on time. Since I was the front man of the Troubadours, that was my job. I was also the one who went to the club owners after the show to get paid. Sometimes, according to where we were, I'd take one of the other Troubadours with me. I remember a club in Brooklyn, New York, where we hadn't drawn very well. Afterwards, I went to get our money from the owner, and he told me, "No crowd, no money."

Well, ordinarily, E.T. would say, "Ahhh, just don't collect it." But this guy was being a real asshole. So I went and got Steve and Wayne—who were both a lot bigger than I was—and they went down into the basement with me to help persuade him to give us what we were owed. It worked, too, although not before there were a few tense moments.

It was a Monday or Tuesday night gig, and I don't think it was even a thousand dollars. Basically, just gas money for the bus. But it almost took a fight to get it.

During the days I was with Ernest, we played on contracts. I don't really remember any times with him where we did deals for the door or anything like that. We had guarantees. And mostly, we got paid cash. Once in a while, if we were somewhere Ernest had played a lot in the past, he'd take a check. Ordinarily, he didn't. It was always green. And by the end of the tour there'd be a suitcase full of cold hard cash riding with us on the bus.

The years I was with Ernest—the latter part of '68 through the first part of '70—I did a little bit of recording as his rhythm guitarist. By that time, Ernest had been making records for some 30 years. He'd had his first No. 1, "Soldier's Last Letter," clear back in 1944, and he'd first cut "Walking the Floor over You" a few years before that.

It had been a great run of hits for him throughout the '50s and most of the '60s, but while his albums were still selling well for Decca, he started having fewer radio hits along about the time I joined him. (I'm pretty sure I didn't have anything to do with that, though.)

I've always thought that the first studio session I played with Ernest included "Saturday Satan Sunday Saint," which was the last of his singles to make the charts in the 1960s. But according to Ronnie Pugh's thorough biography of E.T, *Ernest Tubb: The Texas Troubadour*, which came out from Duke University Press in 1996, that was my buddy Cal Smith, under his birth name of Grant Shofner.

The book lists four sessions that I played with Ernest, all with Owen Bradley producing. The only one that produced a hit was the first, on February 18, 1969, where we cut four tunes with E.T. and Loretta Lynn. One of 'em, "Who's Gonna Take the Garbage Out," went Top 20 for Ernest and Loretta.

The rest of the tracks I did in the studio with E.T. never made it onto the charts, although they did make it onto three Decca albums: *Let's Turn Back the Years* and *Saturday Satan Sunday Saint* from 1969 and *A Good Year for the Wine* from 1970. I didn't sing on any of these recordings; all I did was play rhythm guitar, and you don't want to listen too hard to try and hear me. Like I've said before, I played out of meter, just like Ernest. Ernest, though, didn't play guitar on the recordings, so if you hear a guitarist out of meter on any of 'em, it's going to be me.

I know he let me work with the band in the studio just because he wanted to take care of all the Texas Troubadours, and we got paid for the sessions. He had some good musicians in the band then, but we all got paid whether we were any good or not. Truthfully, at the time it didn't make that much difference. He sold anyway.

I recorded a few singles under my own name during this time. As I've mentioned, I got to work with Owen Bradley, and one of the singles I did with him while I was with Ernest—a Ray Pennington song called "That Big World Out There"—just about broke through nationally.

So the way it looked from the outside, things were going great for B.P. I had a steady job with one of the greats of country music,

I was playing and recording and doing a little bit of stuff on my own. And, truthfully, everything *was* beautiful. E.T. was beautiful, everybody in the band was beautiful. I had no conflicts with anybody. I loved working for Ernest, and with him.

The problem was, I just got tired of the road.

I mean, we'd leave Nashville and go all the way to Seattle, and then start back. We'd go out for days, weeks, without seeing our homes or our families. The more I did it, the less I liked it. So I finally had no choice but to quit.

Ernest understood. He got me a job working with his agent, Haze Jones, booking him and Jack Greene and Cal Smith. The agency wasn't all that far from where we lived in Hendersonville, so I was able to go home and sleep in my own bed every night for the first time in a couple of years.

But as I said at the very beginning of this book, being an agent wasn't what I wanted to do with my life, either. I wanted to get an act booked, all right, but the act I wanted to book was *me*.

Haze Jones was good to me, and the work was all right, but I knew I wasn't going to spend my life calling people on the phone to see if they might be able to use someone I represented for a show at their club or auditorium. I couldn't even see spending a whole lot more time at it.

Then, just as I was wondering what to do next, I got a phone call—and like the one I'd received a few years earlier from Cal Smith, it changed my life.

The Texas Troubadours – 1969
Noel Stanley, Wayne Jernigan, me, Steve Chapman,
and Buddy Charleton. Don't I look good in that hat?

Another 1969 publicity photo of the Texas Troubadours. Me, Noel Stanley, Wayne Jernigan, Ernest Tubb, Steve Chapman, and Buddy Charleton.

CHAPTER NINE

Back when I was on the air at KFMJ, a man named Jack Cresse was one of the salespeople at the station. He was probably the top one, too. Not everyone got along just perfectly with Jack, but we got along real good. He liked me and I liked him.

So I can say definitely that Jack was a friend of mine, even after I moved to Nashville. But that doesn't mean that we were talking on the phone all the time or anything. When you leave a place and start living a different lifestyle—like I'd been doing with Ernest, being on the road all the time—it often happens that you kind of lose touch with your old friends back home. That doesn't mean you don't like 'em anymore or anything like that. It's just changed circumstances.

So while Jack and I were buddies, I have to tell you that I was a little surprised one evening when I picked up the phone and he was on the other end, calling me from Tulsa. That surprise got a lot bigger real quick.

"Billy," he said, "How'd you like to be on a 50,000-watt station?"

Before I could figure out exactly what to say, he added, "Harold Stuart is down in Fort Worth, talking to the owner of WBAP. He's trying to decide about changing KVOO's format to country music. If that happens, we're going to need some people, and the first person I thought of was you."

Harold Stuart was the owner of KVOO, which had long been an affiliate of the NBC network. Its call letters stood for Voice Of Oklahoma, and that gives you an idea about what a big station it was in the market. Around since the mid-1920s, it had been the early home of such famous personalities as Gene Autry, Tony Randall, and newscaster Paul Harvey, but it was best-known as the station that had launched Bob Wills and His Texas Playboys to national stardom in the early 1930s, popularizing the mix of country, pop, blues, fiddle, and Mexican music that came to be known as western swing. At nights, it had a great big broadcast pattern that took in most of the western U.S., plus a lot of other states. Its signal was as strong as its history and heritage.

At the time Jack contacted me, which would've been sometime in the latter half of 1970, KVOO had some real good deejays on the air, playing pop music. Jack Campbell was doing a show, and so was Jay Jones, two good, talented guys who would stay on the air when KVOO did make the transition from pop to country. Jack Cresse, had gone from the sales departments at KFMJ and another local country station, KTOW in Sand Springs, to become KVOO's general manager.

"If we do go country," Jack said, "and I think we will, I'll give you the choice of any shift you'd want—morning drive, middays, whatever."

My mind was racing at the thought of that incredible offer, but I knew right then what I wanted.

"What about the all-night show?" I asked him. "The midnight to five shift."

It was his turn to be surprised. In fact, as I remember it, he told me I was crazy. He wanted me there in the daytime, and he wanted me to be program director.

But doing an all-night show just made the best sense to me. At the time, Bill Mack was on nights at Fort Worth's WBAP—the same place Harold Stuart had gone for guidance about KVOO—and Billy Cole had an all-nighter at WHO in Des Moines, Iowa. Both pure country, and both doing good. Ralph Emery, too, was really established on his late-night show at WSM in Nashville, which was a very powerful station.

Really, though, I think it was Bill Mack more than anyone who made me think about doing an overnight show. He appealed to the long-haul truckers, and that's the same audience I wanted to shoot for. I listened to Ralph Emery and liked him, but I think more about him now as a TV personality. When Ernest and all of us were out in the old Green Hornet, we'd listen to Bill Mack. Ernest would be listening for his latest record, and I'd be listening for mine. Usually, we'd hear his and wouldn't hear mine. But I respected Bill and the way he did the show, and I wanted to have that type of following.

He could also be a little bit of a wild man. One time, he was driving with Ronnie Milsap on the turnpike between Fort Worth and Dallas, and just before they got to the toll gate, Bill switched places with Ronnie so that Ronnie could drive up to the booth. By that time, Milsap had recorded quite a few hits, and anyone who knew country music knew that he couldn't see, so when Bill leaned over from the passenger's side and said, "Meet Ronnie Milsap," the attendant didn't know *what* in the hell to think.

I don't think I ever would've done something like that (even though I've got to admit it was pretty funny). But when it came to the way Bill Mack did his show and how he talked to his late-night crowd, I didn't have any trouble taking him for an example of what could be done with that shift—especially on a strong station. KVOO, with its big 50,000 watts and a nighttime clear-channel broadcast pattern that spread throughout the West, all the way to the Pacific Ocean, would give me hundreds of thousands of potential listeners. A good slice of 'em *had* to be country-music fans. If I could draw a big audience, I figured a lot of artists would come in or phone in from the road and do interviews and that type of thing with me, which would only help me get *more* people tuning in.

Plus, I still loved performing for folks. I wanted to pick and grin and go out and play some dates. Doing the all-night show fit my schedule as an entertainer, and I wouldn't be tied down with any paperwork during the days.

I don't think Jack Cresse had an inkling of just how badly I wanted to get out of Nashville and the booking business. But he did know I was more or less of a proven commodity on the air, and he also knew I could sell ads for whatever time slot I had. You might remember that I sold advertising as well as deejayed when I first started at KFMJ with *The Broken Arrow Hour*. So I was used to selling, and Jack was well aware of that.

He also knew about my desire to keep working in the music business—beyond being a deejay. And he was all for it. He wanted me to keep it up. I think he figured the higher profile I had, the better it was for the station. So my performing ambitions were no problem whatsoever.

Put it all together, and it all seemed too good to be true. But, sure enough, it happened. Harold Stuart came back from Fort Worth and said, "We're going country."

The reason for his decision was simple. That's where the money was.

I should say right here that Harold Stuart was not a country-music fan. In fact, he didn't much like it. It just wasn't his thing, and I sure understand that. When it comes to music, I figure each to his own. But finances and capital were a different story. WBAP was making a lot of money as a country station, and that's what Mr. Stuart saw, and that's why KVOO went country.

—★—

Of course, it didn't happen overnight. In fact, from the time the decision was made, it took a few months before KVOO got all its ducks in a row and the format changed. I knew from experience that getting FCC approval of anything takes a while, and the folks at the station had to have it to make the format change. I'm sure there were other factors, too.

But I couldn't wait—or, I guess, I didn't want to. With the promise of a new and exciting job in my hip pocket, I loaded everything we had in a U-Haul and drove from Hendersonville to Tulsa, with Jerri right with me, driving our Cadillac. In no time, we'd bought a home over on 23rd Street, just east of Memorial Drive, and the three of us had moved into the new place. We hadn't been back in Tulsa very long when our second son, Kris, was born—on February 10, 1971.

Jerri and I were both happy to be back in Tulsa. There was only one thing that kept the situation from being ideal, but it was a pretty big thing: I didn't actually have a job. Not at that time, anyway. Jack Cresse assured me that the all-night show was mine just as soon as KVOO switched formats; meanwhile, though, especially with a new baby, I needed to bring in some kind of income.

Because I'd been in town before and people knew me as a performer and deejay and also knew I'd been with Ernest—all of which gave me some credibility—I was able to start playing out on Fridays and Saturdays. It wasn't long before I was booked just about every weekend. I worked with several different bands during that time, and I traveled out of state some, to Louisiana and Texas, in addition to playing around Tulsa. Haze Jones, my former employer, may have booked some of those dates for me.

Still, I needed something steady—especially, I thought, just in case the unthinkable happened and the KVOO deal fell through. So I went out and got a job at KTOW in Sand Springs, the same place Jack Cresse had gone years earlier after leaving KFMJ. The owner of the station was a man named Buddy Powell. He put me on morning drive, and I started back into the familiar routine of deejaying and selling ads.

It was a long haul then from 23rd and Memorial, where we lived, to Sand Springs; the Crosstown Expressway hadn't been built yet, and you had to take Highway 51 or whatever it was. To give you an idea of how far the station was from our house, we couldn't even pick it up. Now granted, KTOW was low-power, but still . . . I'd do the weather reports, and I'd have to call up Jerri and tell her if there were going to be any storms or anything, because she couldn't pick up our signal. We could get it occasionally at home, when the atmospheric conditions were just right, but not too often.

Man, I'm glad that Buddy Powell is gone now, bless his heart, because I'd hate for him to hear that I'd talked about KTOW that way. But it was the truth. I believe it was the first all-country, 24-hour station in the market, but the signal just wasn't very strong.

Of course, I knew—or at least *hoped*—that my work at KTOW was more or less marking time, just a stopgap until KVOO switched formats and I could take the job Jack Cresse had promised me. But Buddy Powell didn't know it. And when I did get the call from Jack, in August of 1971, Buddy did not take it well. In fact, I tried not to see him after I left because I think he would've tried to whip me.

I really didn't think that I'd been that important to him or the station, but I guess he figured differently, because the day I told him I was leaving he got real mad. I remember that he chewed tobacco and as I explained what I was doing it kind of started drooling out of the side of his mouth and progressed to flying through the air.

So I said my piece, got out of there as quick as I could, and didn't look back.

(The same year I left to go to KVOO, Buddy Powell sold KTOW to a group of investors that included my friends Roy Clark and Hank Thompson, along with Jim Halsey, who had his big country-music agency in Tulsa and managed both of those great country-music stars. Jim told Brett in a recent phone conversation that one of the reasons they wanted the station was that I was on the air there—and as soon as they made the deal, I was gone to KVOO. I'd like to think that was true, but I expect Jim was just being nice.)

Like I said earlier, I wanted the overnight show because KVOO reached so far at night, which gave me the chance to pick up a good national audience. There were a lot of long-haul truckers out there on the highway after midnight, punching the buttons and twisting the knobs on their radios, trying to find something they could get interested in that'd keep 'em awake and alert as the white lines whizzed by. I thought it'd be a good idea to slant things toward that group of folks, many of whom were diehard country fans, so I named my midnight to five a.m. broadcast *The Big Rigger Show*.

I say it was my idea to go after the truck drivers. I guess, like I said earlier, I got the general idea from Bill Mack. By the time *The Big Rigger Show* signed on for the first time, Bill and Billy Cole, the overnight guy out of Des Moines that I mentioned before, had trucker-oriented shows, and so did Charlie Douglas, at WWL in New Orleans. At that time, if you were an all-night jock on a high-powered radio station, those truckers were an important part of your listening audience. When the CB-radio craze came along a few years later, overnight radio shows became less important to the truckers, because they were using their CB's to find out what was ahead and behind them, including info on whether there were any "smokies"—remember their slang for the Highway Patrol?—around.

But when I started *The Big Rigger Show*, that whole CB deal wasn't nearly as big as it got to be. So the truck drivers spent their hours on the road depending on the radio for entertainment, and I tried to make it more interesting for 'em by organizing a group called The Big Rigger Club. If you were a real trucker, you could write in and get a membership card. People could send in requests for cards for their husbands or uncles or whoever, and we'd take those—but whoever got a card had to be an honest-to-goodness trucker. That was the deal. I'd started doing a lot of remotes—live broadcasts from different locations—for KVOO, but I usually didn't take the membership cards. If someone came along and said that he or she was a trucker, or wanted a card for a relative, I'd take the names and addresses and get 'em sent out myself. The truckers also got bright yellow-and-black bumper stickers that read, "I BELONG TO THE BIG COUNTRY! BIG RIGGER CLUB." "Tulsa, Oklahoma" and "KVOO 1170" were printed underneath, along with the cartoon of a tall cowboy hat that was part of the station's "Big Country" branding.

Now, 50 years after I started *The Big Rigger Show*, I can't remember how many truck drivers signed up for the club, but I know there were hundreds and hundreds. Every one of the cards had a number, and on the show I'd call out card numbers and send prizes, usually albums, to the winners. The truckers would call in, too. I'd ask where they were calling from, where they were headed, what the weather was like on their end—things like that. I especially remember one guy stopping and giving me a call from 'way up on the other side of New York City, telling me that I'd called out his Big Rigger number. And you know what? About three days later he drove his big rig to the station and picked up his record album in person!

You never know what would happen on *Billy Parker's Big Rigger Show*. That was a lot of what I liked about it. Unlike the way radio is today, we were just kind of open to anything, entertainment-wise, that might come along. And sure enough, just as I had hoped, one of the things that happened is performers started calling in to talk with me over the air.

Good ol' E.T., my former boss man, was one of the very first to call. Ernest was out on the road somewhere and called in to congratulate me. Just another example of what a classy guy he was. Of course, I was playing him a lot on the show, too.

When John and Brett and I were talking about this part of the book, Wooley asked me if I thought my time with Ernest helped me get the artists on my show. I think his words were, "Did it give you more legitimacy with country-music stars?"

Sure, I guess that's possible. I mean, some of the people I'd been around during my time with E.T.—Cal Smith, Jack Greene, even

Loretta Lynn—would call in pretty regularly. But the truth is, it was the power of KVOO that drew artists to *The Big Rigger Show*, whether they knew me personally or not. I was in a position to get their songs on the air at a 50,000-watt station, one that covered a whole lot of territory and got to a hell of a lot of people. That was the reason performers called me up. It wasn't so much that they wanted to talk to Billy Parker. They wanted to tap into the Big Country radio power that I represented.

In some cases, the calls were prearranged through an artist's management or publicist, but most of the time, they weren't. That makes sense when you think about it. If someone was at home in Nashville, he or she wouldn't really enjoy getting a call at one or two o'clock in the morning. It was different, though, for someone who was out on the road. That's where most of my calls came from. They'd be on their buses, leaving a date in Fort Worth or somewhere, and they'd stop at a restaurant or some other place and phone me. Or they might call me from a club after they'd finished playing for the night. Of course, there weren't any cell phones then, and I don't think any of them had special phones in their buses or anything like that. So it wasn't anything they could do casually. They had to make a point of getting out of the bus and finding a phone before they could talk to you. Remember, too, it was expensive to make a long-distance call then, and a lot of times they'd have to get a bunch of coins so they could feed 'em into a pay phone—just to be able to be on the air with me for a few minutes.

I don't mean to say I got a call from a recording artist every night on the show. But it happened quite a bit.

THANKS—THANKS A LOT

Besides the artists and the truckers, there'd be lots of other people calling on a given night, especially after the all-night show got going good. I'd get a lot of requests—so many that I sometimes couldn't play 'em all—and sometimes people would call up and just want to talk. You know, when you're on the air through the night, you get the kinds of calls you might not get so much of in the daytime. I imagine alcohol has something to do with that, or maybe it's just loneliness, which I imagine gets worse in, as that old Frank Sinatra pop song put it, the wee small hours of the morning. I was lucky, though. Almost from the beginning, I had people who would help me by answering the phone while I was on the air, and that freed me up to concentrate on what I was playing and saying into the microphone.

As you might imagine, I'd sometimes get prank calls. People, both men and women, would identify themselves as this or that country star, seeing if I'd fall for it and put 'em on the air. Most of the time, I didn't. I was pretty good at telling the real stars from the pranksters.

I can't remember who was taking care of the phones on the night someone calling herself Loretta Lynn rang us up, but I believe she was calling collect from somewhere, and that didn't happen very often with music stars. They usually paid for their own calls. (Maybe they were reimbursed by the label. I don't know.) Whoever it was on the phone for me that night held his hand over the mouthpiece and said, "Hey, it's someone calling collect. She says she's Loretta Lynn. Should I accept the call?"

"No," I told him.

So he hung up on her, and we jollied around a little bit about how crazy people were to try and fool us by saying they were stars.

As it turned out, though, it really *was* Loretta. E. T. had told her that she ought to call into my show. And even though I hung up on her the first time, she was nice enough to call back. We had a good visit and promoted her latest record. Sure, I apologized. And I guess the station paid for the call.

Over the years and through all the different time slots I've been on the air at KVOO, I've been lucky enough to have those friends pitching in and answering my phones. It was that way from the very early days of *Billy Parker's Big Rigger Show.* One of the first to help me out was my next-door neighbor in Tulsa, Don Plummer. He'd come up and visit while I was on the air, and he'd end up answering the phone for a couple of hours before heading home. He had his own electric company that he ran during the day, but he found some time to man the all-night-show phones. (Later on, after I got off the all-night beat, he'd become the head man for my golf tournaments, which we'll get into later in the book.)

Another phone-answerer was Tom Carter, who was the country-music writer for the *Tulsa World* newspaper at the time. He'd go on to have a real successful career as an author, writing biographies and other books with—and about—some of the biggest stars in Nashville. He also did a little songwriting; in 1975, while I was still on the all-night show, I recorded one of his tunes called "More Than One Kind of Love" as a single for Sunshine Country Records out of Dallas. He'd come up and visit, sometimes on the air, and he'd answer the phone. I hope Tom doesn't mind me remembering that he usually kept women callers on the phone longer than he did men.

Jim Hardcastle, who owned a place called the Country Corner in Coweta—he also leased the Cain's Ballroom for awhile in the '70s—was another one of my phone guys who enjoyed visiting with the women who called. Later on, I was told that he'd sometimes arrange to meet them at one of the QuikTrips in town. He'd ask what kind of car they were driving, but he wouldn't tell 'em what *he* was driving, so he could go down there and check 'em out. If he didn't like what he saw, he'd drive off. I think he drove off a lot of times.

I remember another clubowner who manned the phone for me. His name was Dennis Dutsch, and he had a place on the outskirts of town called the Party Barn. 'way out on 91st Street between Memorial and Mingo. It was a dancehall that did real good business—especially on Saturday nights, which were always special nights in Tulsa. Dennis would have a lot of different acts come in, usually on Saturday but sometimes on Friday night, too. Later on, my great husband-and-wife friends Roy Ferguson and Candy Noe and I leased the Party Barn from Dennis for awhile. We took it over and paid him rent, and Roy and Candy would play there with their band, the Royals. I'd do some pickin' and grinnin', and we'd bring in national people like Cal Smith, too. At the time, I was working some other dates at various places on the weekends, so I wasn't there *all* the time. Roy and Candy basically ran it.

That was during the time in Oklahoma when the clubs had to be BYOB—bring your own bottle—so we sold ice and setups and snacks. I always accused Roy of eating and drinking up all our profits. After a show, the tomato juice would be gone, and all the peanuts would be gone, and I'd tell Roy we couldn't make any money in this business because of his appetite.

One more story about Dennis Dutsch. He was a pilot, and when Frank Keating became the governor of Oklahoma, Dennis flew his plane. Dennis had also spent some time as a highway patrolman. I'll never forget one Saturday when I was headed out to a show in Pawnee, Oklahoma. I looked up and saw the governor's plane right above me, and not long after that, a patrolman pulled me over and told me I was speeding. I hadn't been, and I knew it. As it turned out, Dennis had set everything up after he saw me out there on the road.

Other people came up and put in time on the request line, too, including my manager and friend Ray Bingham and a young nephew of his named Brett Bingham—the same guy who grew up to be one of the authors of this book.

In addition to the calls, I'd have people come by wanting to visit with me in person. At the time the station was out on Peoria Avenue, and we shared it with what was then KVOO-TV. (Now it's KJRH.) The TV studios were on the ground floor, and we were on the second. There was always a building engineer watching the doors, and anytime someone came by who wanted to come up and be on the show, he'd call me to see if it was all right. Nine times out of 10 it was fine, because they'd made arrangements earlier to be there. It was different if they'd been drinking or something; he could usually tell, and if that was the case, he wouldn't let 'em in—although, I have to say, a few slipped by him every now and then.

You always had to be on the lookout for people who'd been overserved, as the saying goes, just because of the time *The Big Rigger Show* aired. It coincided with the time all the bars closed as well as the peak drinking hours for a lot of folks. I can see where people in that condition might think it would be fun to come up and sit in on a radio show, but the engineer was pretty good about keeping that from happening.

So generally, the all-night show was pretty orderly. I don't remember things ever getting to the point where we had to throw somebody out. About as wild as it got was one night when Gailard Sartain came up. Now, Gailard was a local legend because of his character "Mazeppa," this crazy guy in a big hat and boxing gloves he created for a late-night local TV show. He'd run old movies, and he and his cast would do comedy skits on the breaks. It was real popular, especially with teenagers and college kids. Just about everybody within the range of Tulsa television signals knew about Mazeppa.

In the early '70s, after a couple of years doing the local show, he jumped to Nashville and got a job on *Hee Haw*, the now-famous country-music television program that had just gone into syndication after being on CBS for a couple of years. (I'd end up doing a few guest appearances on *Hee Haw* myself.) Gailard would go on to be a big-time character actor in movies and on TV, but he came up and did the truckers' show earlier in his career. It would make sense that he was on because of the *Hee Haw* connection, but he may not have even been on *Hee Haw* yet. He may have still been Mazeppa.

For whatever reason, he showed up at the door of the building one night and I brought him up to visit. I really liked Gailard—still do—but that evening, he was bouncing off the walls. He had a whistle around his neck, the kind referees use, and he kept on blowing it while we were talking. Gailard thought it was pretty funny, but it got kind of aggravating in a hurry. It made it awful hard to concentrate, and in radio, you've got to always be able to concentrate on what you're doing or you can get into trouble.

I remember the Oak Ridge Boys coming in at around that same time. This was when they were still one of the biggest gospel groups in the country; they hadn't yet made that transition from Christian to mainstream country music. (Jim Halsey, the great manager and agent who, you might remember, was one of KTOW's buyers back in the early '70s, helped them a lot with that.) Best I remember, they'd come to town to play at a church out in Sand Springs, and then they dropped by the studio to do an interview. They didn't sing in the studio—I think they'd done all the gospel singing they wanted to do that night—but I played some of their records and we had a good visit. All four of them—Duane Allen, Joe Bonsall, William Lee Golden, and Richard Sterban—did a great job on the air. They were real personable, and I think you could tell even then that they were going to break out of gospel music and become one of the biggest country acts of their time. They came back on the air with me several more times over the next few years, both as a gospel act and after they'd switched to country, which happened in 1977, while I was still doing overnights.

THANKS—THANKS A LOT

I can't remember that the Oaks ever actually sang live on *The Big Rigger Show*, although they might have hit a note or two somewhere in there. But that was kind of unusual. As the program got more and more popular around the country, it began drawing more entertainers, and a lot of them would bring their guitars in and sing a little bit. I remember Cal Smith visiting the station. And I remember Jack Greene. As I said earlier, those were two of the guys, like me, who were alumni of Ernest Tubb's Texas Troubadours, so we had a lot in common. And, of course, they had records out when they visited, and they figured maybe they'd get a boost with the listeners as well as on the national charts. It was a good situation. Big Country KVOO was a reporting station for *Billboard* magazine, which means that the people there got our playlists and used them to help determine the rankings on their Hot Country Singles chart, which came out weekly. Getting regular spins on *Billy Parker's Big Rigger Show*, or any of the other KVOO programs, went a little ways toward making a record a hit, and don't think the artists weren't aware of that fact.

I had a lot of performers come through during my seven or so years on the overnight show, and two I remember with real good feelings to this day are Barbara Fairchild and Tommy Overstreet. Both of them impressed me not only when they were on the show, but also with their work and just by being the kind of people they were. To me, personality is really the strength behind an artist, especially in the beginning. It means so much. And Barbara really had it, even before those early '70s hits like "The Teddy Bear Song" and "Kid Stuff." I imagine she's still got it.

Tommy Overstreet was just one of the finest people I ever spoke to, on the air or off. He was *sincere*. His music was good. Remember "Heaven Is My Woman's Love" or "Ann (Don't Go Runnin')"? Those were a couple of his big hit records that came out from Columbia in the first couple of years I was doing *Billy Parker's Big Rigger Show*, and I really liked 'em. He could be country, he could be pop, but most of what he did was kind of in a good in-between place. We called him T.O., and he was a *talent*.

In addition to the national recording artists like Barbara and T.O., I tried to make a point of having local entertainers come up and visit. If they had a record, even if it was on some little tiny independent label, I'd always try to give it a spin. Those Tulsa-area acts were a big part of the all-night show. It didn't matter if they were working at the Springdale Tavern or a root-beer stand. It didn't make me any difference. They were in the business, and I tried to help everybody I could.

Some of the local guys I'd played with over the years, people like Johnny Stills and Ted Creekmore, were recording for a Tulsa label called Alvera Records, run by the old western-swing bandleader Al Clauser, and I'd bring 'em in, talk to them, and play their records. I don't know if it did them and their careers any good or not, but I think it made *them* feel good, just to be in the studio and knowing that their music was going out over the air to a lot of different parts of the country, including their hometown.

One of the other local acts I had on a couple of times was Ronnie Dunn. This was several years before he teamed up with Kix Brooks, a Louisiana boy who was also trying to make it as a solo artist. They got together thanks to another Okie named Tim DuBois, the head of the Arista Nashville label, who thought Brooks and Dunn ought to write songs together. But that was several years after Ronnie started coming on *The Big Rigger Show* with me. He was a pretty big club act around Tulsa then, but he wasn't exactly on Nashville's radar yet.

I thought he was a great singer and a good local entertainer, but I couldn't determine at the time whether he'd be strong in the business or not. Of course, he was, and still is to this day.

Later on, when I started working daytime shows, my studio would a lot of times be packed with people, either being interviewed, or performing, or just hanging out. But there weren't that many who dropped into the all-night show, just because of the time we were on. And, like I said, those who did spend time with me in the studio usually made arrangements in advance. We had a chair there for whoever was answering the phone, and if someone came in to visit, I made sure they had someplace to sit down. There was usually a performer, local or national, who wanted to guest on the show, so it was active, but some nights were a lot more active than others.

When I look back on it, I really do think I tried to help everybody in the business that I could. There were a lot of us deejays, I think, who tried to do that, and it's something I don't see too much in today's radio environment. It's a different deal now, a different business model. These days, it's not about selling records. It's all about downloads and live acts. And there are a lot more restrictions, a lot tighter playlists.

Back then, I could play anything that I wanted to—and I did. And Jack Cresse, the general manager who'd put me on the air at KVOO, was right in there with me. We both believed in helping people out, and if someone had a record, even on a tiny little independent label, if they got it to me I would probably play it. Sometimes, it would even go on our weekly chart, *The Big Country Music Guide*, that people could get at record stores and other places for free. We didn't really have any limit to how many songs we put on our Big Country KVOO chart; sometimes, I remember, there were over 100, and there'd always be several on indie labels.

We played a lot more records then than the stations do now, and so we were able to help more artists, whether they were big names or unknowns. That's a big reason why I'm proud of what I did on *The Big Rigger Show*. I really hope what I did for those years of overnight broadcasts was of some little help to the entertainers who dropped by, got their records played, and sat down and talked to me and to all the folks, from truckers to shut-ins to night-shift workers to kids, listening in faithfully from all across America.

It is difficult to pick a place to start my friendship with Billy Parker, because I knew him before we ever sang a country song. He was playing our gospel songs before our music crossed over into country.

When we joined forces with Jim Halsey, five decades ago, Jim told us all about Billy Parker. Billy was so important to the Oak Ridge Boys. He helped break all of our songs and the Midwest followed.

Billy was a writer and singer, but, most people knew him as a great, award-winning, hall of fame disc jockey. I knew him as a good friend. His heart and soul influenced country music that spread from Tulsa to the north, east, west, and south.

Billy was a giant of a character but a very gentle man. Billy was a trusted voice of radio. I am so blessed that our paths crossed and we became good friends for over five decades.

~ **DUANE ALLEN** ~

You can't categorize Billy Parker. Singer, songwriter, musician, for years one of America's important radio personalities. Friend to all. Maybe you can categorize him: all-around good guy.

Billy for decades helped to popularize country music and its artists with his radio shows on 50,000-watt KVOO in Tulsa. The entire music industry owes Billy Parker a debt of gratitude. I'm proud to call him a friend.

Thank you, kind sir.

~ **JIM HALSEY** ~

My mother, Lucille Parker

My father, James Parker

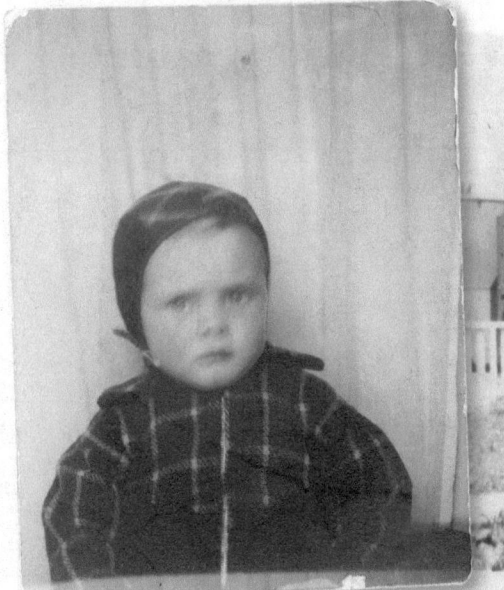

A very young Billie Joe Parker, before I started spelling my name right and before they had good cameras.

THANKS—THANKS A LOT

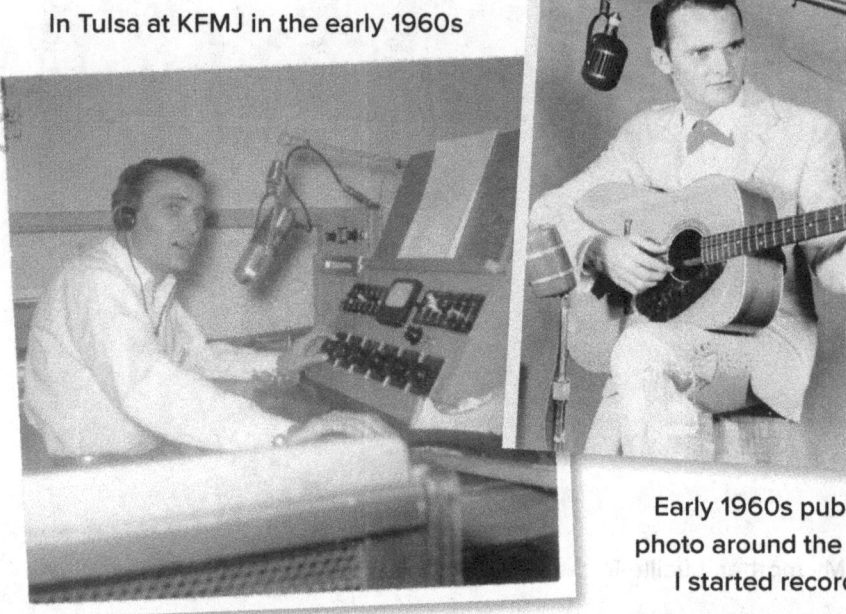

In Tulsa at KFMJ in the early 1960s

Early 1960s publicity photo around the time I started recording.

My mom, me, sister Francis, sister-in-law Betty, brother Jimmy, brother-in-law Richard along with my niece Sharon and nephew Darrell.

BILLY PARKER

These publicity photos from the mid-1960s
became the album covers of my first two albums.

Channel 8 TV Studios – 1962

Me with Wanda Jackson on the Horn Brothers' *Longhorn Wingding*.

Jerry Emery (piano), me (M.C.), J.C. Broughton (fiddle), Jim Carter (bass), "Speedy" West (steel), Don Ramey (drums), Bob Kiser (guitar)

BILLY PARKER

Me and my pal Leon McAuliffe at the Cimarron Ballroom with a representative from Toys for Tots. Leon's Cimarron label would release my original recording of *Thanks A Lot*.

Publicity photos for Decca Records around 1967.

On stage at Cain's Ballroom around 1966 with Rocky Caple on steel guitar, Autry Rutledge on electric guitar, me in my shiny suit, Vernon Walker on bass, and Austin Maxey on guitar. For the life of me I can't recall that drummer's name.

More publicity photos from the 1960s.

With Cal Smith and the great Bob Wills on one of my first tours with the Texas Troubadours.

Me with Miss Jerri Hamblin right around the time she became Mrs. Jerri Parker in 1966.

One of many package shows we did with the Texas Troubadours. Hank Thompson and his band, the Brazos Valley Boys, were on the same show.

THANKS—THANKS A LOT

A couple of family photos with Jerri, Billy Joe, and Kris.

With the CMA DJ of the Year award in 1975.

Doing the Big Rigger show on KVOO in 1971.

THANKS—THANKS A LOT

With my buddy Tommy Overstreet in 1972.

Another of my many hours behind the microphone.

Appearing on *Hee Haw* in 1980s with the great *Hee Haw* band (above) and with Roni Stoneman (below).

THANKS—THANKS A LOT

Me and Merle Haggard – 1992

EZ Chord advertisement

Me at KVOO in 1996.

At one of the Billy Parker Charity Golf Tournaments. I think I looked better than I played.

2003 with my siblings Francis, Oran Lee, and Jimmy.

Billboard congratulations after another Academy of Country Music Award.

CHAPTER TEN

Billy Parker's Big Rigger Show was on the air five nights a week, from early Monday morning to early Friday morning. That gave me the opportunity to work dates on Friday and Saturday night, which I did. I didn't have a band when I first came back to Tulsa, so I worked as a single and sometimes had gigs where local bands would back me. I worked with a lot of house bands around Tulsa, and I'd fly out or drive out to work in Louisiana and different places in Texas. It could be tough, because the band members didn't know me that well and didn't know my songs. Of course, I'd send them my records and hope they'd listen and work up a few of my songs, but most of the time they didn't. So I'd end up doing the country standards and, if I was lucky, a few of my own. Mostly, it was, "Okay, guys, in the key of C," and off we'd go.

I have to say, though, that my career as a picker and grinner wasn't the reason for the Monday through Friday scheduling at

KVOO. It had a lot more to do with the Arbitron ratings. There were separate ratings for weekdays and weekends, and while I never sold a show on the basis of ratings—my thought's always been that if you live by the ratings, you'll die by the ratings—they were important to a lot of people at the station. Weekday ratings just carried much more weight, and so we were a weeknight show.

Back then you could've bought a minute-long spot on *The Big Rigger Show* from me for $25. A lot of times, I didn't go in and cut 'em; I'd just read them live over the air from the ad copy I put together. That was perfect for the all-night shift—it fit right in with the style of the show, kind of laid-back and conversational. Plus, the advertisers liked it because a lot of times I'd talk for two minutes on a spot that was supposed to run a minute. Although I tried to do the same thing after I went to daytimes, it didn't work very good because the program directors put up a lot of resistance about doing spots that way. They were very particular about a thirty-second spot running exactly thirty seconds, and I found out pretty quick that I couldn't get by with the casual way I'd done *The Big Rigger Show* spots.

The Big Rigger Show had lots of sponsors, and it might sound conceited to say this, but once they were onboard, they usually stayed. It wasn't like I had to go out and make sales calls on 'em every day. I never had to beg them to stay on, or try to resell them. Usually, I'd just call 'em up and say, "Do you want to run the same ad this week?" If they did, great. If not, we'd come up with something else.

As you know from earlier chapters, deejaying and selling had always gone hand-in-hand for me. At the time I was doing *The Big*

Rigger Show, I was getting back 15 percent of all my ad sales, which made a good addition to the check KVOO was giving me for my deejay work. Honestly, at the time you didn't make a pile of money just by doing the radio thing—*I* didn't, anyway. So I sold advertising for the all-night show, and then as time went on, I sold for all the different day parts, picking up some great longtime sponsors like the Bill Haynes Company and Ernie Miller Pontiac.

I imagine people might think that selling was the hardest part of what I did during the years *Billy Parker's Big Rigger Show* ran on KVOO. And I guess selling wasn't as much fun as spinning records and talking to artists—although I had great clients and I'm not complaining. But I'm not going to kid you. The hardest part was physical. It was tough to adapt to being up most of the night and sleeping during the day.

For all the years I was on from midnight to five—from August 1971 to late 1978—I hardly ever got the amount of sleep my body needed. Our bedroom was upstairs, and Jerri and I put heavy black shades on the windows so I could sleep in the daytime. So I'd sign off at five a.m. and turn it over to Jack Fox and Otto Dunn, who came on after me. Sometimes, I'd stay up there a little bit with them, just kind of talking and unwinding, before driving home, climbing up the stairs, and trying to relax enough to nod off. A lot of times, I was so keyed up by something or other that had happened on the show that I'd have a lot of trouble just getting myself to the point where I could rest. Even under the best of circumstances, I couldn't sleep past 11 o'clock, or noon at the very latest. So I'd get five or six hours of sleep, maybe, and then I'd be up for the rest of the day, until time to go in and get prepared. I usually was at the studio by about 10 p.m. every night before a show. Sometimes, I might get in a nap at home, but never for very long.

Really and truthfully, in the more than seven years that I did *Billy Parker's Big Rigger Show*, I never did get adjusted to that schedule. That's something that made me admire the truckers, and all the other people listening to me in those midnight hours, all the more.

I said earlier that I wanted to help all the people I could with my show, especially the folks in the business, the local and national entertainers. I'd have them up, or I'd talk to them on the phone. And sometimes, just playing their records was enough to make them grateful.

Back in 1975, a young lady from the little southeastern Oklahoma town of Chockie named Reba McEntire signed a contract with Mercury Records, which was a big deal. Of course, you know that Reba would go on to be one of the true legends in the business. It just took her a little while to get out of the gate.

In 1976, when *The Big Rigger Show* was going strong, Mercury put out her first single, which was called "I Don't Want to Be a One Night Stand." A man named Frank Leffel was the label's national country promotions manager then, and he got the record to me.

Now, I'm not sure why this happened the way it did, but somehow I got in touch with Reba's mother, or she got in touch with me. It might have been because of my good pal Ray Bingham, who started booking dates for Reba around this time. It could even have had something to do with her brother Pake, a bass player and singer I'd worked with and knew.

However it came about, I let the MeEntires know that I was going to play "I Don't Want to Be a One Night Stand" on the all-night show. Besides Pake, Reba's sister Susie also sang—the three of them had started out as the Singing McEntires—and the night I played Reba's single, they all gathered in the family homestead to listen with Mama. Chockie, as you may know, is up in the Ouachita Mountains, and mountains can play hell with a radio signal, so the only place they could pick us up was in their hallway. They all gathered around the radio in the hallway and listened, and then Mama called me up while I was on the air, and she kept thanking me and crying. I'll remember that as long as I live.

"I Don't Want to Be a One Night Stand" only got to No. 88 on the *Billboard* country chart, so a lot of the country never heard it, but the people who listened to *Billy Parker's Big Rigger Show* sure did, and more than once.

Thanks to my buddy Wayne McCombs, the Tulsa entertainment historian I've mentioned before (and I'll mention him again as the book goes on), I recently saw a copy of our *Big Country Music Guide* from September 26, 1975. As I mentioned earlier, this was a weekly chart published by KVOO, letting folks know what was on our playlist at any given time, and that playlist didn't have to have a set number of songs. This one, for instance, listed 96, with Ronnie Milsap's "Daydreams About Night Things," on the RCA label, at No.

THANKS—THANKS A LOT

1. Holding down the very last slot, at No. 96, was "Average Man," on Sunshine Country Records, recorded by a picker and grinner named Billy Parker.

You remember from a few chapters ago that I had my own local label, Pride Records, back in the mid-'60s, recording other acts as well as myself. Somewhere in that era—before I went to work for Ernest in '68—I also put out two albums. As nearly as I can pin things down, both of these came out sometime between late 1966 and the summer of '68, when I headed to Nashville to join Ernest. Both these LPs were kind of hodgepodges, made up of tracks that I'd recorded over the past few years for the different labels I'd been on—including my own. I was just trying to get something out there that people could listen to.

The first one was called *If I Make It Through the Night*, named after that Jeannie Seely tune I'd recorded for 4-Star in '65. Of course, it was the first track on the album. I can't recall how I did it, but I'd gotten permission from every one of those labels to rerelease the songs I'd done for them. So, *If I Make It Through the Night* included Sims releases like "I Hurt Me (Instead of You)," "The Line Between Love and Hate," "Sounds Like A Winner," and a couple I'd done as two sides of a Pride single. It also included "Thanks A Lot."

The identification number for the album is 1001 PLP, which means that it was the first (and only) LP put out by Pride Records. (I think "PLP" meant "Pride LP." I was real clever in those days.) Will Jones, who was a deejay on KFMJ and wrote "Gold Rush Girl," the A-side of my 4-Star single, did the liner notes for me. In them, he said, that much of the success I'd had "can be traced to the Billy Parker Fan Club, Joanne Vogt, President."

Here what I remember about Joanne: She and her mother lived in Broken Arrow and they both loved country music. They were good people and she did do a lot to help me in those early days. It seems to me like the fan club kind of wound down after I left KFMJ.

I did have a second fan club, though, later on. This was after I'd joined up with Ernest, and I can't for the life of me think of the name of the woman who ran it. I believe she lived in Illinois. Just about the only thing I recall about her was a time when she and her husband came to Nashville to go to the Opry and see the Music City sights. I took 'em around, to the *Midnite Jamboree* and all, and they even stayed with Jerri and me one night in Hendersonville. It had to be summertime, because I took 'em both out in my boat. We were cruising along, living the high life, and Jerri, making small talk, said to the woman's husband, "How do you like this boat ride?"

"Aw," he said, "I can take it or leave it."

⸻ ★ ⸻

The second album I did during those pre-E.T. days was called *From Me to You*. Like *If I Make It Through the Night*, it's a bunch of stuff I previously released. The liner notes start with the first line of the theme song I had at KFMJ—"It's Billy Parker, comin' your way!"—and go on to say: "This is the little tune that greets thousands upon thousands of Country Music lovers who live within the 8,000,000 acre listening area of Radio Ranch, KFMJ in Tulsa, Oklahoma."

(You don't want to look too closely at that 8,000,000-acre ranch figure. With 640 acres making up a square mile, by my calculations that would've translated to 12,500 square miles-- five times the distance between the East and West Coasts, or about halfway around the world. KFMJ had a pretty good range, but it damn sure wasn't *that* good.)

There's a lot more to the notes, including an acknowledgement of my band, led by Rocky Caple, listed here as the Shot Guns (two words instead of the usual one), and an endorsement from David Ingles, my good friend, the KFMJ deejay who played piano on "Thanks A Lot" and also had his own label.

From Me to You came out from a label called Luck Records, which I think I started after Pride ended. It has two of the songs I'd recorded earlier as a 45 for Pride, "I Fall in Love Too Easy" and "Just Enough" (misprinted as "Just English" on the album jacket), both written by Dave Burgess and produced by David Ingles. Dave, I believe, was with a band called the Champs, who'd had that big instrumental hit "Tequila," in '58. (They were on the Challenge label, which was owned by Gene Autry, and I've heard that the Champs were named after Champion, Gene's horse in the movies.) I know Dave wrote other songs for country acts, but I don't remember how I got his songs to record. It could have had something to do with 4-Star, which was distributed by Challenge.

The LP included the flip side of the single I'd done for Russell Sims's label in 1964, that weird little tune "Tatooed Lover"; my original "Out of Your Heart," the flip side of Cimarron Records' "Thanks A Lot"; and another that I'd put out as the A-side of a single under the Luck name, "Lots of Luck." (Come to think of it, maybe that's where the name of the label came from.) "Lots of Luck" was written by the co-writer of "Thanks A Lot," Eddie Miller.

As it turned out, the label might've been named Luck, but it didn't bring me any luck on the national charts. None of those songs, or any of the other tunes I'd cut on various labels, made any noise for me nationally. "Thanks A Lot" had come pretty close, back in '63, but Ernest's version had smothered mine. And those Decca sides I talked about earlier, produced by one of the biggest names in country music, Owen Bradley and released during the time I was with E.T., didn't chart either, even though there were pockets of the country that played 'em a lot.

I'm not going to lie to you: What I'm telling you about these records isn't just from my memory; Brett and John have been doing a lot of research into those old discs and letting me know what they've found. And as often as not, I get surprised.

Here's an example. In 1972, a Nashville label called Metro Country put out a single on me: "When You Speak to the Kids" b/w "Leave All the Lovin' to Us." (the B-side was a play on the Greyhound bus advertising line that said, "Go Greyhound, and leave the driving to us.") According to the label, it was distributed by Starday—the label that Pappy Daily, the Texan who put out my first records, had helped start—and produced by Gary Paxton, who also co-wrote the A-side.

Gary Paxton was just about as famous a producer and studio guy as Owen Bradley. Among a lot of other things, he was responsible for a couple of the biggest rock 'n' roll hits ever recorded—"Alley Oop" and "The Monster Mash." In 1971, he'd had a religious conversion and gone mostly into Christian music, but before that he was doing a lot of stuff in Nashville, and he kept his hand in country even after going gospel. In fact, he'd written and produced Don Gibson's No. 1 hit, "Woman (Sensuous Woman)," the same year I cut "When You Speak to the Kids." I'd played the Don Gibson song a lot on *The Big Rigger Show*.

From everything I can gather, Gary Paxton was quite an unusual guy, the kind of person you'd remember meeting. But I don't recall anything about the sessions for the record, or even meeting him. I think I recorded it somewhere besides Nashville— most likely Oklahoma City, for reasons I'll talk about in just a minute—and Paxton may not have even been at the sessions. But I just don't remember anything about how or where that record was cut.

Then, in '74, I did a single for a label called Artco. I'd kind of forgotten about it until my co-writers brought it up, and then I found my copy and Jerri and I sat down and listened to it for the first time in a *long* time. It made me cry. It wasn't because I sang it so well or anything like that. It was just a beautiful song with some strong lyrics, like, "Bring back those days when we had nothing, nothing but our true, true love."

That was the name of the A-side: "Nothing (But Our True Love)." Both it and the B-side, "Now She's Just Mine," were written by . . . Gary Paxton.

I vaguely recalled someone sending me a demo for those two Paxton songs from down the turnpike in Oklahoma City, and maybe recording them later in OKC, but that was about all.

Then John and Brett kept on digging, and they found out that the label, Artco, was based out of Oklahoma City and run by a man named Tom Hartman, who'd been a publisher at Tree International in Nashville and had a gospel label as well. He also had a recording studio in OKC. They ran down a story about Artco in a copy of *Billboard* magazine from November 9, 1974 that talked about Tom's talent roster, which included the famous Oklahoma actor Dale Robertson, the cowboy-music veteran Jimmy Wakely, and another actor, James Brolin, who was a pretty big movie star at the time, along with acts named Arbuckle, the Uptown Bluegrass Boys, Red Pony, and The Bluegrass Okies. According to the story, Artco had even released a record featuring the mandolin playing of Nudie, designer of those glittery "Nudie Suits" worn by people like Porter Wagoner and Elvis. (Actually, Nudie had released it on his own label, Nudie Records, but Artco surely had something to do with it.)

Once I heard his name again, I realized I knew exactly who they were talking about. I just hadn't thought about Tom Hartman for many years. A heavy-set, jolly guy, he was a nice man and very good to me. I'm sure we got acquainted when I had the truckers' show.

Piecing things together, we figured that Tom Hartman was connected with Gary Paxton through Tom's time in Nashville or his work in gospel music, and it was maybe even Tom Hartman who had contacted me to do the 45 that came out on the Metro Country label. That seems right to me. And while neither one of those records did anything much nationally, I'm proud of those collaborations with Gary Paxton—now that I've discovered them again.

I have to say, though, that there were a lot of songs I recorded that I never sang on stage. Those Paxton songs fall into that category. I went into the studio, recorded 'em, and when they didn't hit, I went on to something else. So maybe I can be forgiven a little bit for not being able to remember all I should about them.

I don't mean to say that *any* of the songs I recorded became super hits. But they did start showing up on the *Billboard* country charts in 1976, not long after *The Billy Parker Big Rigger Show* got going. Like "Average Man" and the song Tom Carter wrote, "More Than One Kind of Love," the first ones were all recorded for Sunshine Country Records, run by a good guy out of Dallas everybody called the General. His name was Bart Barton, and we became acquainted when he came up to KVOO to promote one of his Sunshine Country discs. I don't know who specifically he was promoting, but there were plenty of candidates. Another *Billboard* story—this one from September 7, 1974—carried an ad from Sunshine Country, with the slogan "Country and Proud of It" and a list of acts that includes John Wells, Bobby Dee Trimm, Pat McCurdy, Ed Landry, and a singer who went by the one-word name Fargo. Most of those were Dallas-area entertainers, I think, but a story accompanying the ad says that Bobby Dee Trimm was from McAlester, Oklahoma and Pat McCurdy was discovered at a talent show in Norman, Oklahoma. So there were some Okies on the Sunshine Country roster, too, myself included.

Later on, the General would sign my great pal Curly Lewis—the fiddler and vocalist who'd been with Hank Thompson, Leon

McAuliffe, and Johnnie Lee Wills—as well as Candy Noe, Roy Ferguson's better half. The best-known Okie that recorded for the General was my friend Carl Belew, who'd cut the hits "Hello Out There" and "Am I That Easy to Forget"—and, if you remember, wrote the one called "Baby I'm Gone" that I did for BTR Records in Tulsa back in '67.

In addition to being one of the Oklahomans on Sunshine Country Records, I was also one of at least three disc jockeys the General signed up. The other two were friends of mine: Charlie Douglas, out of WWL in New Orleans, the guy behind *The Road Gang* overnight truckers' show, and Dugg Collins out of Amarillo, who was a big name in country radio at the time. In fact, he'd be named Disc Jockey of the Year by the Country Music Association in 1979.

You know as well as I do that a label like Sunshine Country and a businessman like the General saw advantages in giving deejays recording contracts. Dugg and Charlie and I may not have been the most talented or most powerful singers you could get, but we had followings in the country-music field. At that time, in the mid-'70s, people knew who we were, and recognition is worth a lot in this business. A lot of people were listening to my doggone show.

There's something else, too. If you were a deejay, you'd have a tendency to play a record by someone who was on the same label as you. I don't ever recall being pressured by the General, or by any of the other label guys I recorded for, to play a particular act on my show. But I played 'em. Then again, like I said earlier, if a record was decent, I'd give *anyone* a spin or two, especially since no one ever told me what I could or couldn't do on the all-night show. I knew what was hot and what people wanted to hear, but the final call was up to me, and I made room for everyone I could.

Having said that, I have to also say that I didn't play my own records very much. I played 'em some—I won't lie—especially when one came along that I really liked or thought was extra good. My fellow deejays at KVOO were real nice about giving me spins, which of course put my records on the *Big Country Music Guide*. As you probably remember from what I said earlier, we were a *Billboard* reporting station, so me getting played on KVOO helped my chances when the national charts got put together.

Even though it never went national, I imagine I played "Average Man" a few times on *Billy Parker's Big Rigger Show*. That may even be why it made an appearance at the bottom of the *Big Country Music Guide* from 1975 that Wayne McCombs showed me. A songwriter named Don Wayne, who wrote two of Cal Smith's biggest hits—"Country Bumpkin" and "It's Time to Pay the Fiddler," both from '74—did that one, and I've always identified with those lyrics about being "an average man, doing the best I can with what I've got."

But as much as I liked it, it never cracked the *Billboard* country singles chart, and neither did several other tunes I did for the General's label. Finally, in 1976, I charted for the first time nationally with a cheatin' song called "It's Bad When You're Caught (With the Goods)." The next year, I had another small hit with "Lord If I Make It To Heaven Can I Bring My Own Angel Along," which is still one of my favorites, mostly because it describes so well how I feel about Jerri.

Both of those songs were written by my pal T.O., Tommy Overstreet, and his songwriting partner Dale Vest. They were two of the four songs I recorded in Nashville for the General; most of the time, we cut my Sunshine Country stuff in Dallas. And while they both only climbed up into the seventies on the Billboard Hot Country Singles chart, they got played a lot around this part of the country—enough to get me some bookings in Texas and Louisiana, in addition to the dates I was doing in Oklahoma.

From my days at KFMJ, Ray Bingham had always helped me with bookings, and I'm sure he had something to do with lining up those out-of-state appearances. But I think a lot of it was just kind of through me. The General wasn't a booking agent. He just did the records. But he liked going with me to shows. I remember driving down to Dallas to meet him, and the two of us going to Louisiana for me to play some dates.

I worked a lot around Texas then. One of my memories is making the acquaintance of a performer named Bob Luman when we both played the Longhorn Ballroom in Dallas. That was the club built for Bob Wills and His Texas Playboys back in the early '50s, after he'd left KVOO; then, it was called the Bob Wills Ranch House. Bob Luman may not be too well-remembered today, but he was one of the greatest entertainers I've ever seen. I was working mostly off the regional strength of "Lord If I Make It to Heaven" at the time, and I can't remember whether I followed him or he followed me onto the Longhorn Ballroom stage. Either way, he was a tough act to share a bill with, because he had so much charisma and talent. I didn't know how I could stand up to what he did, but I had to, so I guess I did all right. It wasn't like I had any choice.

I think that the two other songs I cut in Nashville for Sunshine Country were "If You've Got to Have It Your Way (I'll Go Mine)" and "What Did I Promise Her Last Night." Both of those made the lower part of the national charts, but you probably know the second one better as a big Mel Tillis hit from 1977—the same year I cut my version. In fact, mine came out in September, and his came out in November, just two months later. He might've already had his in the can when mine was released, but once again, I got covered like a blanket. He just covered the fire out of it.

Between "Thanks A Lot" and "What Did I Promise Her Last Night," I've been covered just about as much as anybody in the business, and I guess I could have let it discourage me along the way. But this is how I looked at it: If other people are getting hits with songs I've recorded, it must mean that I have a pretty good ear for picking material.

> *You've made a huge difference in my life. You were the very first one to play my first single, "I Don't Want to Be a One Night Stand." I'll never forget being in the house there at Chockie where all of us kids grew up. We had the radio on and we were listening for it night and day and you came on the air and said, "I want to play this brand new single from a little old red-haired girl from Chockie, Oklahoma."*
>
> *Billy, thank you so much. Mama, Susie and I cried right there in the hall of our house and I'll just never forget it.*

BILLY PARKER

You're a very special person and you've done so many things for so many people. I'm proud to call you my friend and I'm glad to be your friend. I love you with all my heart.

~ REBA McENTIRE ~

(from the 2005 Billy Parker radio tribute)

Pake McEntire and me

In the late 1970s, I was playing bass and singing at the W H Corral Dancehall in Sulphur, Oklahoma. One Saturday night Billy Parker was booked in there, with us as his backup band. I stood way back on the bandstand, in front of my amp, giving Billy plenty of room to work the show. But he went back there and pushed me to the front, where he was.

When we took a break, he said, "Don't you be a bit bashful in this business. People are going to compare you to Reba as long as you play and sing. But don't hang your head to anyone."

I am a firm believer that when it is all said and done in this life people will not remember how much money we have or how much fame we had. What they will remember is how you made them feel. Every time I'm around Billy he makes me feel special.

~ Pake McEntire ~

CHAPTER ELEVEN

Not too far back in this book, I said something about remotes. When I was doing *Billy Parker's Big Rigger Show*, remote broadcasts were a big part of radio, and they could be pretty lucrative, too. What happened with a remote was that a business paid for you to come out and set up and do your show from there—from a remote location, which is where the name comes from. You'd talk about where you were, and what specials they had for listeners who wanted to drop by, and so on, and just hope that people showed up and bought whatever it was the remote was trying to sell.

Offhand, about the only remote I can recall is one I did at the Sears store out in Whittier Square, which was a big shopping center out on Admiral and Lewis. One of the things you do at a remote is talk to the folks during the times your records are playing, and a woman came up to me and asked if I knew her husband. She gave me his name and I said, "Oh, *sure* I know him. You tell him I said hello, all right?"

"I can't, Billy," she said. "He died several months ago."

I was so embarrassed. I guess I've never exactly gotten over it, since it's what came to mind when Brett and John asked me about remotes. They all kind of blend together for me—automobile dealerships, department stores, big truck stops, visiting with people in all sorts of different situations.

Luckily, Wayne McCombs came through once again, this time with a couple of memories about big remotes he and I did together. He told me that in '74, Bill Mack—who you remember had his all-night show over WBAP in Dallas, which helped influence me to want to do overnights on KVOO—and I joined together to do a remote for Transtar trucks at the Union 76 Truck Stop in Catoosa, just outside of Tulsa. That was a huge place, very popular with truckers coming in off the Turner Turnpike and down I-44, until 1993, when a tornado tore it to pieces. Wayne, who was working at KVOO then, said I asked him to engineer for me, and at one point he looked at the board and thought, "I've got 100,000 watts of power right at my fingertips." That was true, too—KVOO had 50,000, and so did WBAP.

A couple of years later, in spring of '76, Wayne had left the station to work at an advertising agency. One of his clients was a new car dealership out on 11th and Harvard called Bob Drewell Dodge. As Wayne remembered it, they wanted to make some sort of splash, to let people know about 'em, and he came up with the idea of me doing a *Big Rigger Show* remote from there.

They were pretty hesitant to do it, Wayne told me, simply because they didn't think anyone would go out and buy a vehicle between midnight and five a.m. But he talked 'em into it, I went out and did the broadcast, and according to Wayne, they sold a dozen cars during the time I was doing the remote, and they were amazed that they did.

It was during the years of *Billy Parker's Big Rigger Show* that I got lucky enough to start winning some big awards. The first one came along in 1975, and in many ways it was the top honor I've ever gotten: Disc Jockey of the Year, as voted on by the members of the Country Music Association. What made it even more of an honor to me was that I was only the second person to get it; the CMA had starting giving them out just a year before. It was a one-time-only deal, too. Once you got it, you could never win it again.

I feel sure that Bill Mack won it that first year, but Brett and John haven't been able to track that down. I do know that I got mine at a hotel—Spence Manor, I believe—down in Nashville during the annual DJ Convention. The convention was a part of Fan Fair, that yearly celebration that lets fans meet their favorite country stars.

A big deal for all of us who worked in country radio, the DJ Convention went all the way back to 1952. Here's what the country-music historian Byron Fay wrote about it on his *Fayfare's Opry Blog* (Fayfare.blogspot.com):

> Originally known as the DJ (Disc Jockey) Convention, it was organized to honor the Grand Ole Opry while consolidating Nashville's role in the country music industry. The event,

which originally commemorated the Grand Ole Opry's Birthday Celebration, was suggested in 1951 by Harianne Moore of WSM's advertising department. The idea was for the country music artists to thank the disc jockeys for playing their records and promoting their concerts, while giving the disc jockeys the opportunity to meet the stars and to tape spots with the artists to be played on their local stations.

As time went on, the CMA took over the DJ Convention and made it part of Fan Fair, which drew a ton of people to Nashville. The entertainers that came out for the event didn't just mingle with their fans—during the DJ Convention, they spent time with us, too, so it was someplace you wanted to be if you were in radio.

I think I'd already been notified that I'd won Disc Jockey of the Year before I actually went to Nashville; as nearly as I can remember, it wasn't one of those things like the Oscars, where they have several finalists and nobody knows who's going to get one. I remember sitting down there in the front row of that hotel ballroom, nervous as a cat, Jack Cresse beside me. We'd flown down together. There was a really big crowd, mostly people like me who had their own radio shows, and even though I knew whose name was going to be called when the award was announced, when it actually happened and I heard "Billy Parker" from the platform up front, it still kind of shocked me. I wish I could tell you what I said in my acceptance speech, but I honestly just don't have any idea. I just remember looking out over that full ballroom at the folks clapping, all their eyes on me.

Like I said, that was the first big award I got. Later on, mostly while I was with *The Big Rigger Show*, I won four Disc Jockey of the Year awards from the Academy of Country Music, the other major country-music organization, based in L.A. (Unlike the CMA award, you could be the ACM's Disc Jockey of the Year more than once.) I flew out to get those, too. I remember taking a plane to the West Coast with Jon Stuart, Harold's son, once, and going out there with Jack Cresse other times.

The first three were for 1975—the same year I got the CMA award—1977, and 1978. The last one came in '84, after I'd switched to days on KVOO and become both music director and program director. By the time that one came along, the ACM had started giving them out according to the size of the station's coverage area. In '84, KVOO won Medium Market Radio Station of the Year at the same time I got ACM's Disc Jockey of the Year for Medium Market.

I'll talk more about my switch from nights to days in the next chapter, but I'd like to close this one out with a couple of thoughts about these honors that were given to me. At the time they started coming, to be truthful with you, I couldn't believe that out of all the people who were up for the awards, and all the people in country radio across the whole U.S.A., that I'd ever win *anything*. And I know the reason I did was all because of KVOO. I mean, I hadn't won any awards *before* KVOO, and I haven't won any *since* KVOO.

I always give credit to the radio station that was my home for so many years, because when you get right down to it, I don't think I was all that different from anyone else who was on the air. I really mean that. I had good ratings on the overnight show, but the reason I got 'em had an awful lot to do with all the territory that KVOO's signal covered.

These days, people take a lot of things for granted when it comes to the entertainment business, whether it's radio, or television, or music. I guess it was the same when I was coming up and doing all the stuff I did. But I can truthfully say that throughout my career, no matter where I was or what the situation happened to be, I've always been very thankful for the people who helped me do the best I could as a deejay, a performer, an entertainer. I really can tell you that during all those years I was on the air and cutting records and playing dates, I never took *any* of it for granted.

And you know something? I still don't.

KVOO General Manager Jack Cresse and me with the 1975 CMA DJ of the Year Award.

BILLY PARKER
SOMETHING OLD SOMETHING NEW

CHAPTER TWELVE

You know, in a lot of ways I really dug my years of doing *Billy Parker's Big Rigger Show.*

I loved the artists who took the time and effort to call in from the road, and it made me feel good to think that I was making the miles go by a little faster for truckers across the country. I loved and appreciated the friends who came up to the studio and helped me by answering phones. With maybe one or two exceptions, I loved all the local entertainers who came up to do interviews with me. And it was good to think that I helped them a little, too, by playing their records and giving them some time on a show that had a pretty big bunch of listeners out there in radio land.

But, as I said earlier, there were some problems with working all night, five days a week, and trying to catch up on my sleep while the sun's rays came full-blast around the edges of the black window shades in our bedroom. After Kris came into the world, in February of '71, Jerri and I had two young boys at home, and because I had to come home and sleep for part of the day after working all night, I wasn't getting as much time with them as I thought I should have.

I did the *Big Rigger Show* for more than seven years—or, to look at it another way, the better part of a decade. I don't want to say it was getting old, or *I* was getting old, but I felt like I'd been doing it for a good long time when I finally left it and switched to days.

Really, the honest reason I left the all-night show wasn't because I was tired of it, or even just plain tired after working nights for so long. I *was* a little worn out from it, I'll admit; those hours have a way of grinding you down. But the reason I finally went to daytime was because of one man: Jack Cresse, the guy who'd brought me to KVOO in the first place.

From the very first, when he'd called me down in Hendersonville and asked if I wanted to be on KVOO if it went country, Jack had wanted me to have a daytime show. He had what he figured was a good reason. If I had a daytime air shift, I could also be the station's music director—something I couldn't do as long as I was working nights. To be honest, music director wasn't a job I was particularly hot to have at the time, but Jack reduced my hours on the air so I could take care of it. That took a little pressure off me, family-wise, because I went to more or less "normal" hours.

When I first left the all-night show, the only time I was actually on the air was from 9 a.m. until noon, Monday through Friday. That was a little more than half the time I'd been at the microphone for *The Big Rigger Show* every weeknight. But even with those reduced hours, I was still working full-time, because Jack not only made me music director, but operations director as well. Plus, I was still doing sales, just like I'd done from the very beginning of my radio career.

I admit that I haven't kept up with the latest happenings in radio all that well, but I do know that if you tried to be both of those things in this day and age, radio people would think you were nuts. But that's what I did for years in the second phase of my life at KVOO, and it wouldn't have happened if Jack hadn't believed in me, trusted me, and had faith in what he thought I could do.

While the three of us were working on this book, Brett asked me the difference between the jobs of music director and operations director. I told him that the operations director was responsible for all the on-air personnel at the station, including the newscasters and the deejays. That meant that whoever had the job did both the hiring and the firing for the station—and I was that guy. Jay Jones was our program director when I started, meaning that he was in charge of what we aired, how much news and how we presented the music and so forth—our programming. Technically, I was his boss, but we worked side by side on a lot of things, especially when it came to the people we had on the air.

My other title, music director, made me the person responsible for the records that the jocks played, for picking the songs that got on the KVOO charts we put out every week. Those listings of what we played went not only to places around Tulsa where listeners could pick 'em up, but also to the people at *Billboard* magazine who compiled the official national country-music charts. It wasn't all that easy to sort through all the 45 rpm records I received and make those decisions, because there was an awful lot of country-music product being released then. I knew, too, that behind every single record was an artist and other people who wanted to do anything they could to make it a hit. And back then, you could sum up the difference between a hit and a flop in one word: airplay. If you got on the air—especially at a big clear-channel station like KVOO, which took you to a lot of parts of the country—then you had a chance.

"So," Brett said, after I explained the difference in the two jobs, "the artists sucked up to the music director, and the employees sucked up to the operations director."

I thought that was a pretty funny way of looking at it, but he was also exactly right. Maybe "suck up" is kind of an extreme way to put it, but the artists and promoters and label people *were* interested in getting my ear when I was KVOO's music director. Once again, it wasn't because of Billy Parker. It was because of KVOO, which I think was one of the top 10 of all the *Billboard* reporting stations, where Billy Parker happened to be the music director. We were a 50,000-watt station that was respected by the industry, and at that time, like I say, radio *made* artists. I'm not just talking about KVOO; I'm talking about the whole radio industry. If enough stations played their record on a regular basis and reported that airplay to *Billboard*, they became stars. In fact, if you liked an artist and thought he or she had a lot of talent or a real good song, you might even report that the record was doing a little bit better than it was actually doing, just to help out.

BILLY PARKER

Back in those days, when you had the opportunity—like I did and like so many more in radio did—you helped out.

~ ★ ~

Because radio airplay, especially on powerful stations like KVOO, was a big factor in boosting an entertainer's visibility, there were those who tried to get a leg up on the competition by doing something illegal, or at least unethical. I'm talking here about "payola," which has been around the industry, I guess, ever since radio started playing people's records. Payola means that someone offers a deejay money, or gifts, or even royalties on a song in exchange for making sure a certain record gets played. Payola, really, is just another word for "bribe." The U.S. Congress passed some laws to try to stop it in the '60s, and a few radio-station people lost their jobs over the years when they got caught doing it, but when I was at KVOO it was still going on. I suspect it still is, even if radio doesn't mean nearly as much to show-biz careers as it did in my time.

I'll tell you the truth: When I was music director, I did have people come to me and offer me money to play a new single. One time, I remember, it was a guy from Colorado—I've forgotten his name—but he was real insistent about it and couldn't understand why I turned him down.

I did, though. I just wasn't going to accept it.

There were lots of reasons, but one of the biggest had to do with me being a picker and a grinner as well as a disc jockey. I knew, from an artist's standpoint, how hard it was to get airplay. I really didn't get much of it until I got with Ernest, and then with Decca.

That's when radio-station people started knowing my name a little bit and playing me some.

But there in the beginning, even though I was trying hard to get my stuff played, I *never* offered anybody any money to put my song on the air. Of course, I didn't have any money then, anyway. Still, even when I was first cutting records and having a hard time getting any disc jockeys to play me, it would've made me mad to think I'd had to bribe someone to get my record played on the air. To me, airplay like that wouldn't have been *real*.

So I think the fact I worked both sides of the street—the artist side and the deejay side—helped me resist any payola offers that came my way. That doesn't mean I wouldn't let a record promoter take me to lunch every once in awhile, like my friend and former co-worker at KVOO, Mike Wilson, who went on to a great career representing major-label artists. When I was music director, he'd come through and take me over to the Celebrity Club or wherever. He wasn't the only one who did that, either.

So maybe I'm guilty, after all—of taking "foodola."

When I first left the overnight show, in late '78, CD's weren't around yet, and they wouldn't take over for a few more years. The way songs came to you then were through those 45 rpm records and vinyl albums. As music director, I always had stacks of those 45's people were pitching to me, hoping to land on our charts. Of course, they couldn't all make it.

I've been asked a thousand times how I chose the songs that

went on the air at KVOO, and I always say it was determined by ear. I don't mean that I just listened to the song, although that was real important, because you didn't ever want to put a real clunker on the air. But it was also about listening to the record-label promoters when they called you up from Nashville or wherever—or, sometimes, even dropped by the station.

I had one day a week that I set aside just to take calls from promoters. On that day, anybody was welcome to call. The big majority of the calls were from promotion people, affiliated with record labels that were big and tiny and in-between. Occasionally, I might also hear from a lesser artist who was trying to get on the charts, but never from a Waylon Jennings or a Willie Nelson or a Merle Haggard. I spent most of those set-aside days talking to promoters, and while I heard enough b.s. to fill a hundred pastures with plenty left over, I never put anybody down, record-wise. I never told a promoter that his artist was terrible, the song was bad, or the production was lousy. There were lots of stinkers, sure, but I knew even the worst-sounding artist in the world was trying hard to make a good record.

After all was said and done, I determined whether we'd play a song by judging whether or not it was something I thought our listeners would like. If I didn't think it'd work for KVOO and I knew I wasn't going to put it in rotation, I'd sometimes just tell the promoter that our charts were loaded, but maybe next week. Even though in those years, as I said earlier, we'd have as many as 100 songs on our playlist, there were 'way more records being pitched to the station than we could put into any kind of rotation.

Being in rotation, in radio terminology, meant that a record was played regularly on a station. *How* regularly was determined by its position on the charts, which was in turn determined by the jocks and me and audience feedback on songs. So if a song was real popular, in the top 10 or top 20, it would be in what we called heavy rotation, which meant that you'd hear it on KVOO more than you would another single that was maybe only in the forties or fifties on our chart. There was light rotation, medium rotation, and heavy rotation, and the last one was what every artist and promoter wanted.

I mentioned audience feedback. You had to understand about that, especially when it came to artists with local ties. Let's say there was a Tulsa singer named Peggy Jones who cut a record, and it wasn't too bad, although it wasn't too great, either. Just like on the *Big Rigger Show*, we might have her come to the studio and visit and play her song on my program or someone else's. That would be a one-time deal. But then, maybe Peggy's mom, and her sister, and her cousins—none of them telling us who they are or anything—start calling up and saying how much they love that new Peggy Jones record and could we please play it some more. We always expected that, and if we got a lot of it we might play the song a time or two more, because we were pretty lenient in those days.

If it wasn't a very good record, though, I might just play it once. I had to use good discretion, because every song like that I played took the place of another one that people were really wanting to hear. So if it was below our standards, and relatives or friends of the artists—or even the artists themselves—called me up wanting to know if I was going to put it in rotation, I had to say no. I'm sure

I went through some people who really disliked me because they thought I was standing in the way of their stardom. Truthfully, it was usually that the record just wasn't good enough to get anywhere against its competition for the charts. Even though I really did try to help everybody, I couldn't please 'em all.

Thinking about all of that makes me remember that it wasn't just unknown or beginning or wannabe artists—along with friends and family members—who got upset with me when they thought I was shortchanging them on airplay. It even happened with the biggest-selling country-music act that ever hit the charts.

Well, let me change that a little. It wasn't Garth Brooks who got mad at me—or maybe *he* did, too, now that I think about it. But the one I remember who got *really* angry towards me was his mama, Colleen.

This happened a little later on in my career, a couple of years after Mike Oatman and Mike Lynch and their Great Empire Broadcasting had bought KVOO from the Stuart family. It was late in 1992, and Garth, who'd gotten hotter than a depot stove, had his very first Christmas album out. Well, you know, there are tons and tons of Christmas songs, and our policy was to only mix in a few with our regular playlist, so there was a lot of competition for those spots on the KVOO airwaves.

I'll tell you the truth: I may have played cuts from that CD once or twice, but I didn't play them very much, because I just didn't think they were as good as most of the other holiday songs we had. So I didn't really push that album. Garth was and still is a great talent, and I'd had the privilege of working with him when he was just starting out and liked him a lot. I just wasn't a big fan of his first Christmas record.

I'd known Garth's mother real well many years ago, when she was Colleen Smittle. 'Way back before KVOO, and even before Ernest, she and I had worked Jump's Roller Rink in Fairfax, Oklahoma, every Saturday night, both of us singing. Her husband then, Jim Smittle, played the fiddle. She was a great friend of mine—until we got crossways, all those years later, because I didn't play Garth's new Christmas songs enough. She got mad at me over that CD, and she stayed mad. Some years later, before her death in 1999, we reconnected a little bit, and she came up and did my show. She was nice and all and we had a good time talking about the old days, but I could tell she was still a little upset with me.

It's too late for Colleen, but I'd like to think that some other folks who got angry with me back then and have continued to think poorly of me for not playing a song enough or doing enough to help a career may be reading these words right now. I know there are still some people out there who think I done 'em wrong just because I could, because I was throwing my weight around or thought I was a big deal or something. That never happened. I really did try to help everybody I could. There just wasn't room on the charts for all of 'em to go into rotation on KVOO, and I always, *always* had to go with my ear.

The promotion people I dealt with weekly were mostly down in Nashville. A lot of them would have four or five singles and artists they were representing. Some were affiliated with the big labels, like MCA and RCA, and some were independent record producers promoting their own recording artists. I remember Gene Kennedy, who had a little label called Hickory Records, and when he'd call up music directors he'd not only be representing Hickory, but also other independent product.

No matter the size of the label or the stature of their artists, the promoters' pitches were always pretty much the same. They'd ask if I received their act's latest record, and I'd either tell them I had and we'd started playing it or I'd say something like, "Hoss, I received it but I haven't listened to it yet. I'll be listening to it this week, so let's talk about it next week." I didn't know everything about every single record that came across my desk, but I did know that if they were calling about a new one from Waylon Jennings or Merle Haggard, people like that, we'd be playing it as soon as we got it. In those cases, I could give them reports about where it would probably be on the KVOO charts the next week, and that information would help them figure where it might land nationally—or, if it had already charted in *Billboard*, whether it was headed up or down.

I might say something as simple as, "Oh, yeah, we're playing it and it's looking good." To help me get a handle on particular singles, I might ask 'em what kinds of reports they were getting from other stations. Of course, they'd usually tell me it was the hottest thing since sliced bread. I had to keep a lot of this stuff straight in my mind and learn what and who to trust.

Another thing that happened is kind of an inside-radio deal. I imagine you have to spend a little time in the business before you realize how one act could be pushed over another one, even when they were on the same label with the same promoter hyping them. On any chart—and, once again, even KVOO with its hundred or so slots was no exception—the space was limited. Like every other business, the labels were about money, and their big acts were the ones that were making them the most money. So, it was in the labels' best interests to get records by their superstars as high on every chart as they could—even if it meant sacrificing one of their artists who wasn't quite at the same level.

One good example of this was "Hard Hat Days and Honky Tonk Nights," a great song by my pal Red Steagall that came out in 1980—at about the same time his label, Elektra, released one on Hank Williams Jr., who was red-hot at the time. The label threw its weight and resources behind old Bocephus, and kind of hung Red's song out to dry. It's as good a real country song as you'd ever want to hear, and it was a natural tie-in to the movie *Urban Cowboy*, which came out the same year and had that exact phrase, "hard hat days and honky tonk nights," on its posters. You remember how much that film influenced country music (maybe not for the better, but that's another story). Still, even with all of that to help it along, Red's single stalled out at No. 30 on the *Billboard* country singles chart.

The promoters didn't really make any attempt to hide this tactic. I remember one of the Columbia guys telling me, "Hey, Billy, Tommy Overstreet's single isn't making it this week, but we've got a new single out on so-and-so. So listen to that one—and you can kind of ease off on Tommy's and take it down a notch." That kind of thing happened all the time, and I know that's the reason a bunch of artists didn't get any higher on the charts than they did—or didn't even make the charts at all. Hell, I was probably one of 'em, when I was on Decca in the late '60s, at the same time as Jack Greene, Cal Smith, and E.T. The label wasn't going to push me ahead of any of its star artists.

That one day a week was my day set aside for promotional calls, but people would sometimes try to get hold of me on other days. The ones who came by the station to see me personally would usually try to time their visits so they could catch me just after I got off the air. Those were the promoters, and sometimes artists, who did it the old way. Remember the film about Loretta Lynn's life, *Coal Miner's Daughter*? There were scenes of her out on the road with a box full of records, back when she was just starting out, dropping them off across the country at whatever stations would let her in the door. A few people still preferred to do it like that.

One of the guys I especially remember who'd always rather talk to me face to face was Frank Mull, who later on became Merle Haggard's manager. Seems like he was coming through all the time with maybe two or three records he was promoting. There were several others like him, good promoters, who just preferred to do their business in person instead of over the phone. These were some of the same guys I mentioned earlier, the ones who always wanted to take me to lunch.

Like I said before, it was a lot easier to give a record at least *some* air time back then. I've never really thought much about it, but I guess I brought my philosophy from *The Big Rigger Show* to my job as music director. If someone came along with a new record, no matter who it was or how big or small the label, nine times out of

10 I'd give it a spin or two. If I wanted to be honest with myself, this probably had to do with the fact that I was kind of in the recording business, and wanted to be in it a little more. Because of that, I always had a deep feeling for people who were in the same kind of situation. Good local people like Roy Ferguson and Candy Noe, Ted Creekmore, Johnny Stills—if they had a record out, I'd play it. I think that's another thing you couldn't do in the business now, and it's too bad. Everyone who cuts a record has a dream, and while I knew then I couldn't make anyone a star by myself, I could damn sure get their record on the air once or twice at a big country-music station. And a lot of times, that was a big part of their dream.

I don't know if that's still true for the people coming up today, since the role of radio has changed so much. But I hope it is, and I hope there are still deejays who are willing to give new artists and indie labels a little bit of a boost.

You can bet I still had my own sweet dreams when it came to records, even after all the years I'd spent in the business and seeing what went on behind the curtain, like they say in *The Wizard of Oz*. By 1979, when I went from nights to days, I'd recorded a couple of dozen tunes, with a few making a little noise on the national charts. At the time, Bart Barton, the General, was still putting out records on me through his Sunshine Country label.

Early in that year, the General wanted me to do an album, and he brought me to Dallas for the recording sessions. I was really surprised at one of the tunes he asked me to cut down there.

"Why record that one?" I thought. "Ernest already had it out, and it did good for him."

But the General wanted it, and he was in charge of the sessions, so I did it. As you've probably guessed, it was "Thanks A Lot." He knew I'd recorded it in the sixties and thought it might be time for another go-round.

I guess he was right, sort of. When it was released as a single, in July of '79, it did get played on several stations around the country, enough that it got up to No. 80 on the *Billboard* country chart. So even though my version had been covered like a blanket by both E.T. and Brenda Lee in the '60s, before my Cimarron Records 45 could go anywhere, Billy Parker's "Thanks A Lot" finally became a little bit of a hit.

I can't say it enough. Then, radio play was the ultimate thing for someone who wanted to be a nationally known country artist. You couldn't get off the ground without it. The idea was to get noticed by a record label, get signed, and get your song on the radio. Even an independent label had a chance of making an artist into a national star.

I can't say I was ever a real recording star, but at least people kept trying to make me one—and I did hit the charts pretty regularly for about 10 years, starting back in '76 with "It's Bad When You're Caught (With the Goods)" for Sunshine Country. In early '81, a producer out of L.A. named Ray Ruff brought me to California to cut a single for his label, which was called Oak Records. I believe the B-side was a new version of "Lord If I Make It to Heaven," which had become my signature song by that time. But the A-side, the song promoted to radio, was called "Better Side of Thirty." It had an uptempo beat and I wasn't sure it was my style, but it did okay, getting up to No. 74 in *Billboard*.

That was the only record I ever cut for Ray Ruff, whose label had started out in Christian music and then expanded. He recorded a lot of folks, but his biggest record was probably an EP he put out a few years after "Better Side of Thirty." It was called *Guitars Cadillacs Etc. Etc.*—the first album by Dwight Yoakam.

Once again, I know that I got connected with Ray Ruff because of KVOO. Several of us deejays from around the country, affiliated with big clear-channel stations, probably seemed like a good bet for independent labels. Because of our stations, we had a little bit of name recognition. Plus, in my case, I was music director for a big *Billboard* reporting station, and that couldn't hurt, either, when the label was looking to get airplay for its singles.

I guess most of my success as a recording artist came in the '80s, after I signed with Soundwaves Records. It was one of the labels distributed by NSD, Nationwide Sound Distributors, out of Nashville. In doing their research for this book, Brett and John found a story about NSD in the September 13, 1975 *Billboard*. Here's a part of it, which ran under the headline "Indie Distrib Boom Flourishing":

> NSD, formed in 1972, represents 25 labels and such artists as Roy Head, Wilma Burgess and Bud Logan on the Shannon label, Tommy Jennings on Paragon Records and Ruby Falls on 50 States.

Other labels being distributed by NSD are Sound Waves, Phono, Resco, Black Stallion, Brand X and Sun Flower Records.

Headed by Joe and Betty Gibson, NSD has 10-15 releases a month with 50 percent of its product making the national charts. They have grown from a one-man operation to 10 full-time employees.

The same year I started recording for Joe and Betty, Soundwaves would release what I believe was the label's biggest hit. I'd like to say it was one of my records, but it wasn't. It was a novelty tune, previously released on a couple of small labels, called "Grandma Got Run over by A Reindeer." The Soundwaves release took off during the holidays in '83 and you still can't miss hearing that song every Christmas season.

My own records for Joe and Betty Gibson's label never made it to anywhere near that level, but I got to record some good tunes for Soundwaves, and several of 'em showed up on the charts pretty regularly over the next few years. None made the country Top 40, but I got fairly close a few times, especially in the spring of '82. That's when the label released a great tune by Buddy Brock Jr. called "(Who's Gonna Sing) The Last Country Song." I say "great" not because of my performance—it was just a really good song with strong lyrics and some first-class harmony vocals. Produced by Joe Gibson, it was credited on the 45 label to "Billy Parker and Friend"; that friend was Darrell McCall, who's still a great vocalist and songwriter. At the time, he'd been with some big labels—Atlantic,

Mercury, RCA, and Columbia—and he'd had a Top 40 duet hit with Willie Nelson with a remake of the Bob Wills western-swing hit "Lily Dale." Our own duet on "(Who's Gonna Sing) The Last Country Song" just fell short of the Top 40, officially coming at No. 41. That would be my high-water mark on the *Billboard* country charts.

Darrell, who I'd work with again on a Bob Wills tribute album I did in the '90s for my old friend Russell Sims, also sang harmony on the follow-up single to "Who's Gonna Sing," which came out in March '82. It was called "If I Ever Need A Lady," and Joe and Betty Gibson put it out in June of '82. It also charted, but not quite as well.

Both of those songs were from a Soundwaves LP named after our single, *(Who's Gonna Sing) The Last Country Song*. It was one of two albums that I recorded during a trip to Nashville in the early '80s. A pair of my good musical friends from Tulsa, Johnnie Lee Wills and Roy Ferguson, went along with me and ended up appearing on some of the tracks, along with a whole studio full of Nashville A-team pickers. Those guys, people like Buddy Spicher and Jimmy Capps and Pig Robbins—they were thrilled to death to have Johnnie Lee there. I believe that the most conversation in the whole session centered around Johnnie Lee. Everybody wanted to meet him and talk to him.

Betty Gibson, I'm pretty sure, was the one who got hold of Darrell McCall for the project. I knew Darrell, too, and I'd played a whole lot of his music on my radio shows, so of course I wanted him to be on the album. He also appeared on my second Soundwaves album, *Something Old, Something New*, which was full of duets with other country performers. Betty chose a couple of people she wanted for the project—Bill Carlisle and Jimmy Payne—and I came up with the rest. Some of them, like Jack Greene, Cal Smith, and E. T. himself were guys I'd gotten to know before and during my time with the Texas Troubadours. And I admired Webb Pierce from his early years in the business.

As I said, I'd brought Johnnie Lee Wills down with me from Tulsa; he was the only one of the featured duet singers who didn't live in or around Nashville.

Johnnie Lee, Roy Ferguson, and I had a lot of fun redoing two big western-swing hits, "Take Me Back to Tulsa" and "Milk Cow Blues," with that great band of studio musicians. Funny enough, both of those songs were first released in 1941, about 40 years before we cut our versions. "Take Me Back to Tulsa" had been a big record for Bob Wills, and "Milk Cow Blues" had done real well for Johnnie Lee. One of the things I remember best about the two duets with Johnnie Lee is how we kidded one another on the mike while we were recording. A lot of our back-and-forth made it onto the final cut.

There wasn't any kidding with Webb Pierce, though. We did a new version of his hit from the mid-'60s, "Memory No. 1," for the album, and when he came into the studio he was fighting a cold, so he had his cold medicine with him. At least, that's what he called it. We started in, with him singing harmony, and when we got to the bridge there was a place he couldn't reach, because the cold had messed with his sinuses and his throat. He just couldn't get there, vocal-wise.

Finally, I said, "Webb, why don't you just do the straight part, and I'll sing the harmony."

Boy, that made him *mad*.

"Hell, no," he said. "I can get it!" He was determined to hit that note, and he did. You can hear it on the record. He was so put out that I have no doubt he'd have kept us all there until he got it right—no matter how long, or how much cold medicine, it took.

I really loved working with E.T. again. We cut a duet on a song he wrote with Johnny Bond—the pride of Enville, Oklahoma—that had been one of Ernest's first real big records. It was "Tomorrow Never Comes," first released in 1945. Only a couple of years after he and I did that session together, we'd lose Ernest, but at the time he was still out there working on the road. It was an honor to not only sing one of his earliest hits, but also to have him join me on the session.

These days, it can take a long time to do an album, with all the tweaking and stuff that goes on in the studio. But back then, there wasn't much to it. You just went in and did it. Of course, it helped to have pros all around me, from the Nashville session guys to the great artists who sang with me.

Out of all of them, the only one who had any trouble, or said anything that was even a little negative, was Webb Pierce. But, like I said, he got the job done. Darrell McCall didn't say anything at all during the sessions, good *or* bad, but that's because he wasn't there. He added his parts later on, and everything he did was just right.

A song I did with Darrell for *Something Old, Something New*, called "Love Don't Know A Lady (From A Honky Tonk Girl)" made the national charts in the spring of '83. A few months earlier, another single from that album, "Too Many Irons in the Fire," got up there a little bit for Cal Smith and me.

(Who's Gonna Sing) The Last Country Song was the first of the two albums to be released. The Gibsons put it out in '82, following up the next year with *Something Old, Something New*. In the late '90s, Bear Family Records out of Germany put the two together in a CD package, changing the title to *Billy Parker & Friends*. Last time I looked, it was still for sale.

Of course, the records were only part of it. Playing live was just as important in terms of getting your name out there and entertaining the folks.

When I came back to Tulsa in '71, after leaving Ernest, I was working shows as a single. I didn't have a band of my own, but I'd work some with different groups, especially when I was playing jobs around Tulsa. As time went on, I got to where I'd be working again and again with a couple of those bands.

One was Stonehorse, a great western-swing and country group that Ray Bingham booked and managed. They'd started out as the Country Cousins when they were mostly just kids, and they matured into a real good band that played all over the country, including a long run of 10-day bookings every December in Las Vegas, performing in conjunction with the National Finals Rodeo. All of 'em—including Reba's brother Pake McEntire, who was a member before signing his RCA Nashville deal in '86—were just top-notch; their drummer, Darlene Passmore, was one of the finest I ever heard, and one of the few lady drummers I ever worked with. She's still a super friend of Ray's and mine. So are the rest of the members of that band: Donnie, Dale, and Brenda Talbert and Mike and Brent Self. One of the band's fiddlers, Mark McClurg, left in the early '90s to go with Alan Jackson; he's still got that gig. He's also still married to Brenda Talbert.

You may recognize that "Self" name from earlier in this book. Remember Frances Self and the Playmates, one of the bands I worked with a lot early on around Tulsa? Louie Self, Mike and Brent's father, is a first cousin to Frances. So is Margie Talbert, mother of the three Talberts who were in the band. So I guess you could say I've been working with the Selfs almost since my career started; on top of everything else, it seems Stonehorse and I were *always* playing KVOO's listener-appreciation events. And I was proud to have 'em on stage with me. .

Really and truthfully, that was the most *prepared* bunch I ever saw. If I had a new song out they needed to learn, I didn't have to worry whether they'd be able to do it or not when it came time. They'd run it down in the right key, figure out the harmonies, and all I'd have to do is slide in behind the microphone and make sure I remembered the words. It was a solid, solid band, and just another example of how Ray Bingham, from the very beginning of my career, was the foundation for everything I did in the business.

The other group I worked with a lot was called the Silver Dollar Band, and there were some great guys in it, people I'd known and worked with for years, including Rocky Caple, Billy Dozier, Claude Clemons, David Thayer, and Clarence Boyd. Clarence and his son, Dewayne—a good bass player and singer—owned a big place called the Silver Dollar Ballroom in Kellyville, about 20 miles south of

Tulsa. Of course, the Silver Dollar Band was the house group there, and I played there a lot with them. (Later on, beginning around the late '80s, I worked a lot of dates with Candis Clark and the Blue Ribbon Band—which had Rocky, Claude, and David in it.)

We also did a TV show, for a while, at Tulsa's biggest dancehall, Duke's Country. It was in the early 1980s, when that whole Urban Cowboy thing was going so strong, and it was done for a new UHF station called KOKI, Channel 23, which had signed on in 1980 and was looking for programming.

David Thayer, who was the Silver Dollar Band's lead guitarist, remembers Channel 23's *The Billy Parker Show* very well—a lot better than I do, frankly. When Brett talked to him about this book, David told him that we all had to show up around six p.m. on the day of the taping, and we might not get done until midnight or one a.m. because the production crew wasn't the most experienced and had to do a lot of retakes. David remembered that each band member made $60 per show, which didn't seem like a lot for all the time they put in, but he also said that I somehow negotiated with the producers and got 'em all residuals, since the show was syndicated to other UHF stations around the country. (There were live audiences for the tapings; I don't think they got anything except a little live entertainment.)

"We got $30 every time it was re-aired," David told Brett, "and sometimes I'd go to the mailbox and it'd be full of $30 checks from all the stations that had picked it up."

There's a little bit of stuff from those shows out there on YouTube and Facebook, and that helped jog my memory about *The Billy Parker Show*, which David thought ran for about 15 weekly episodes. In one of those clips, I'm introduced by our announcer, Lynn Waggoner from the Oklahoma City radio station KEBC, and run up through the crowd to the stage wearing two pieces of clothing I almost never wore when I performed: a big cowboy hat and an *apron*, which I throw off once I start singing "Pick Me Up on Your Way Down" with the band.

Now, even though I'd hated wearing a hat when I was with Ernest, I recall that I *did* wear a hat for a little while when I was working solo. I just don't recall the reason. And I've got no earthly idea why I had on an apron. One of our sponsors was James Country Style Sausage, and I'd do live commercials for them, so maybe the apron had something to do with that. (One of the commercials is on YouTube, with me singing a song about their sausage and telling folks how "the James boys use choice cuts of pork, then blend in their secret seasoning.") The main sponsors were Getty Refining and Marketing Company, and their local Skelly stations and Skelgas propane dealers, and IT—In-Home Theater, a subscription satellite-television service that beamed movies and special programming down to its customers.

It was kind of funny how the show was set up. I'd do a song or two with the house group—the Silver Dollar Band—and guest stars from around Tulsa would come on and also play live with our group. I believe Candy Noe and Gayla Earlene, whose husband played steel guitar, were regulars, and then we'd have folks like John D. Levan, a popular nightclub performer around Tulsa, and a good singer named Lori Lynn, from Cushing, come on and do a number with the group. By this time, Jana Jae had become well-known in the country-music world as a regular on the big syndicated show *Hee Haw*, but she lived in Tulsa and came on at least once to play her fiddle with our group. (You can see her in one of the YouTube clips, and John D. and his wife, Chris, singing "Storms Never Last" in another.)

Each week, we'd also feature Nashville acts like Crystal Gayle, Razzy Bailey, Kenny Serratt, and Tommy Collins. I'd sort of *suggest* that they were appearing on the Duke's stage in front of our crowd, but the truth was that they were really in videos that had been taken during live performances somewhere else. I don't know if we fooled very many people, but we did give 'em some good music.

I imagine that whole Urban Cowboy thing was one of the reasons *The Billy Parker Show* got its shot, along with the fact that Channel 23 was a new station looking to make a splash. I'll never know how many people saw it, because I don't know where all it was syndicated, but I think we did get a lot of viewers.

Back in the '60s and '70s, there were a lot of syndicated country-music TV shows out there. A lot of times, stations would use 'em to fill out their programming on the weekends. Even people who weren't country-music fans then remember *The Porter Wagoner Show*, for instance, with Dolly Parton talking about how you couldn't buy the beautiful towels she was showing you; you could only get 'em in boxes of Breeze, the laundry detergent that was one of their sponsors.

Although I can't remember for sure, I don't think I ever was on Porter's show. But I remember appearing on what amounted to a spinoff of that program. The Wilburn Brothers, Teddy and Doyle, had started out on *The Porter Wagoner Show*, and then they'd gone on to start their own syndicated series. During the time I was with Ernest and recording my own stuff on Decca, I did *The Wilburn Brothers Show* several times. YouTube's got the clips to prove it. And boy, do I look young in 'em.

There's a clip or two out there of me on *Hee Haw*, too, which was the very biggest of all the syndicated country shows; after starting out on the CBS TV network, it ended up running for more than 25 years, which is probably some kind of record for a country-music series.

Best I can remember, I appeared on that program two or three times. Once, I sang "Thanks A Lot" with that great *Hee Haw* band, and I got to do some of the comedy stuff that they set up every week, with people popping up in the cornfield to tell jokes. In fact, I did a salute to my hometown of Tuskegee with Roni Stoneman, a cast member who was probably best known for her comedy character Ida Lee, who'd chase men around, trying to catch 'em with her butterfly net. I don't remember her chasing me, though.

Hee Haw was recorded in segments. So I'd go in when they told me to and do my songs with the band. They'd shoot all those back to back, just like they shot the cornfield scenes, and put it together later. So I was never there at the same time Roy Clark and Buck Owens, the two hosts, shot *their* stuff.

Nashville Now, Ralph Emery's TV show, was another big country program at the time, and I did it several times. Ralph was always good to me, and I figured it was worth it to my career to drive or fly down to Nashville just to appear with him, especially when I had a new single out. I'm sure both *Nashville Now* and *Hee Haw* sold some records for me, and I still appreciate being asked to do both those shows, which were the top television showcases for a country performer then.

I also should mention the program I hosted for Stan Hitchcock up in Branson, Mo., when he had the Americana Television Network going there. That was in the early '90s, when Branson was really hitting on all cylinders when it came to live entertainment. Stan was a big radio and TV guy and had some hit country records as well—remember "Honey, I'm Home," from the late '60s? Right before starting up the Americana Network, he'd been at CMT in Nashville. He'd helped start that one, too. He left after Gaylord Entertainment bought it and headed to Branson.

I hosted a show for Stan called *Branson Backstage*. He produced it. I'd go up to Branson and stay for about a week or a week and a half each time we shot and go to the different venues to interview the entertainers there. That was a time when Branson was exploding with all kinds of different entertainment—especially country music. Roy Clark had been the first country star to get his own theater in Branson, back in '83, and when it was successful, that opened up the floodgates for a lot more big-name veteran country acts to come in. So I went back a long ways with a lot of the people I interviewed on camera for Stan's TV show. I always enjoyed going up there, renewing acquaintances, and swapping stories about the business, and I appreciate Stan Hitchcock for giving me the opportunity to do all of that for his television network.

I wrote earlier about how Ray Bingham was my foundation, and it's true. Another thing he did to help me and my career was book big shows with maybe four or five hot artists—recording stars like Moe Bandy and TG Sheppard, who were two of my very favorite people—and then add me in as a part of the show. These would be in big halls like Tulsa's Expo Square Pavilion, Maxwell Convention Center, and the Oral Roberts University Mabee Center. Most of the time, I'd come out first, sing a song, and then emcee for the rest of the night.

I did a lot of that over the years, and KVOO encouraged it, since it didn't just raise the profile for me, but for the radio station as well. Usually when I worked as an emcee, I didn't charge either the station or whoever booked the show. It was great publicity, the kind of publicity I couldn't have bought for any price—associating me with the biggest artists in country music. Like my deejaying on KVOO, doing these concerts really helped me from the standpoint of exposure to big audiences that loved country music. During this time, Ray was one of the top booking agents and producers in the United States, and he sure did right by me.

He still does.

There are so many things I could say about my great friend Billy. I think the most important one is the way he treats people. No matter who you are, he'll always make you feel like you're his very best buddy. I don't know how many times I saw him bring total strangers into the broadcast booth to do his show. He didn't only make them feel at home; by the time they were done, they felt like they were being inducted into the hall of fame.

BILLY PARKER

I'm proud of Billy for a lot of reasons. I'll always be especially proud of him for being so kind to everybody, no matter what their circumstances or walks of life.
　　　　　　　　~ **RAY BINGHAM** ~

My respect and admiration for Billy Parker cannot be adequately stated with words. Billy Parker has supported me as an entertainer for almost 50 years. He played my records on KVOO every time I released one. Over the years we developed a friendship that I treasure with all my heart. We have shared a million laughs as well as an affinity for blackberry schnapps. However, we only got in trouble with it once.

Billy truly is my hero and special friend. I look forward to our ponies making tracks on the same trail for years to come. RIDE HARD COWBOY.
　　　　　　　　~ **RED STEAGALL** ~

Ray Bingham, me, and Red Steagall – 2005

One of the publicity photos done for the Bill Haynes Company.

CHAPTER THIRTEEN

Except for moving to a daytime shift and becoming music director and operations director at KVOO, my life in the late 1970s and early '80s stayed pretty much the same. In 1984, I even won the last of those four Disc Jockey of the Year for Medium Market awards from the Academy of Country Music—the only one I got after I left *Billy Parker's Big Rigger Show* for the daytime gig.

At home, our two boys, Billy Joe and Kris, were old enough to be in school, and outside of the home I was still plugging away with records and personal appearances, as well as continuing in sales. I'd been selling ads from the very beginning, when I got that part-time spot on KFMJ, and I continued when Jack Cresse brought me back from Tennessee to be on KVOO. That made me a little unusual. The other more or less national overnight guys at the time, like Bill Mack and Charlie Douglas, didn't sell their own advertising, but I did. When I moved to days, I kept selling spots for my own show. I've always liked to say that I kind of sold myself into the radio business. KVOO was paying me both a salary and a commission on my sales, and the two together made us a pretty good living for that day and time.

Because of my being in sales and the relationships I built, I came to be associated with several different advertisers—who also became my friends. I've been lucky enough to know some great ones over the years, like Roy & Candy's Music and Gilbert's Audiology, just to name two who were with me for a long time.

Then there was my special friend Bill Haynes, owner of the Bill Haynes Company in Tulsa. Sometime in 1979, after I'd gotten off the all-night show, Bill approached me about becoming the spokesman for his company, which specialized in storm windows and steel and vinyl siding. Honestly, at that time, the siding and window business didn't have the best reputation, and you didn't want to jump on board with just anybody. But when I looked into it, I saw that Bill was an honest, respectable man who ran an honest, respectable business. And once I started working with him, I never saw one thing that made me even consider changing my mind.

In addition to advertising on my KVOO show, Bill started putting me in TV spots. Then, he'd buy television time on Sunday afternoons and sponsor a movie, which I would introduce. As I recall, we started with John Wayne pictures and switched to other action movies when we ran out of his films. In addition to coming on at the beginning, I'd try to sell folks on Bill's products with spots between sections of the movie. I remember once we played the front part of a movie, and I came on with a pitch for the Bill

Haynes Company, and then somehow when we went back to the film it had gotten out of order. We played the last part of it in the middle and the middle part of it last. I'll never forget the calls we got from people, just raising hell about it.

We gave some of my singles and albums away on these shows and in other sales promotions, and Bill had some pictures of me made up with the Bill Haynes Company logo at the bottom. I'd go out with Bill on some of his calls and autograph photos for the people we were visiting. He'd introduce me to a potential customer, then I'd sit there and listen to Bill's presentation; I heard it so many times that I could have done it myself, pretty much word for word.

Those sales calls could be interesting. I remember one particular place where he'd sold some siding, and while we were all there talking a bunch of chickens ran in from outside, through an open door, and squawked and flapped right past my feet.

Joe Moore was a third-generation funeral director—his grandfather, uncle, and dad had established Moore Undertakers 'way back around 1900. By the time I knew him, he was the owner of Moore Funeral Homes in Tulsa, another good and another reliable advertiser on KVOO. Joe was one of the friendliest guys I've ever met, one of the nicest people as well, and he loved Bob Wills and western- swing music. That's how I got acquainted with him. I would say that he became one of the best friends I've ever had, and I'm happy to say that his son, Dr. Joseph Moore, and his family are also good friends of mine.

Brett reminded me about the song his friend Rich O'Brien wrote called "They've Taken Bob Back to Tulsa," which is about bringing Bob Wills's body up from Texas to be buried at Tulsa's Memorial Park Cemetery. Back in the early 2000s, when O'Brien's song came out, Brett brought it in to me to play on my show, and we talked about how Joe Moore was the one driving the hearse carrying Bob's remains, and how he and Betty Wills, Bob's wife, listened to KVOO on the way up from Fort Worth. That would've been in 1975, and they were driving at night, so they would have been listening to my all-night truckers' show. And I'm sure I played a Bob Wills tune or two that night.

For many years, I did a *lot* of remotes from Claremore, just about a half-hour northeast of Tulsa on old Route 66, for my good friends Dave and Gloria Pierce. I also did a lot of radio and TV for 'em. They'd moved here from back east—I believe they were in New York—where Dave had been a mechanic. So he knew a lot about the business, and it showed in the way he ran Dave's Claremore RV. I got a lot of my RV's from them because I knew they could be trusted. They were just good people, good to me, and their daughter Stephanie is cut from that very same cloth. She came up with her mom many, many times to do my show. I like to think that she learned a little bit about radio and TV from me. I *know* I learned from her. It didn't take me long to see that she was as good at doing commercials for 'em as I was. I always knew that she'd be professional every time she came up. For years now, she's been in charge of Dave's RV, and she's doing a real good job with their advertising.

Ernie Miller at Ernie Miller Pontiac-GMC was another great advertiser and friend, and after he passed, his son Marc was good to me, too. You remember earlier on in the book, when I talked about doing a TV show back in the '60s for Ray Bradley Chevrolet. Ray and Ernie Miller were great buddies over the years, and when Ray Bradley got out of the business, I guess you might say that Ernie took me over—and I'm sure glad he did. I was associated with Ernie for decades, doing both radio and TV for him. I remember that when his salesmen made their quota on sales, he'd send them to Hawaii, or on an Alaskan cruise, and he'd ask me along, too. That was just one of the ways he went out of his way to be good to me.

Another great thing Ernie did was furnish me with new Pontiacs to drive. One Saturday night I took a new car he'd loaned me down to the Green Country Ballroom in Poteau, where I was playing a job with the house band. A man named Dale Holcomb and his wife ran the place, and they were known for the big crowds they drew every Saturday night. This Saturday was no exception, even though it was wintertime and cold, with an icy rain falling.

My buddy Jack Fox, who had the morning show on KVOO, was just about the country-music-lovin'est guy you'd ever meet, and he was from the country around Poteau, so he came out to the show that night. Jack took his own car, and my friend and neighbor Don Plummer and I drove down in the Ernie Miller Pontiac.

When I was done for the night and out in the parking lot, getting ready to go home, I suddenly realized I'd locked the keys in the car. Several of us were out there looking over the situation when Jack stepped up.

"Don't worry about it," he said. "I'll get 'em out of there."

Next thing I knew, he had a screwdriver and a little hammer, and he was saying, "I'll just make a little hole here so we can fish out the keys, and then you can go on." He hit the window, once, and the whole dadgum passenger-side glass shattered.

Don Plummer drove the car all the way back to Tulsa, and I sat on the side where it was broken out, holding a towel up to keep the rain from hitting me in the face and trying not to freeze to death, all thanks to the "little hole" Jack Fox made.

I've said before that everything in my career—pickin' and grinnin', playing on stage, joining up with E.T., making records—all gets back to radio, and especially to KVOO. For many years I was in a position to help people because of what I did on the radio, and during that time there were people who were in a position to help *me*, too. I made a lot of friends and a lot of business connections because of my years at the microphone and my experience in sales.

I've been lucky enough to be the spokesman for several great businesses, like the ones I mentioned just a little bit ago. Of course, there were lots of others I worked with over my years in radio, and maybe I was just lucky, but I had good experiences with just about every one.

I say "just about." Very occasionally, someone would come along, buy a bunch of advertising from me, and then, once the ads had run, leave KVOO and me holding the bag. The biggest one that comes to mind is someone I actually knew. In fact, I'd known him for a long time, since my Red Foley and Ozark Jubilee days. He'd been with Red for years before getting his own band.

When he came to me, he was involved in a mobile-home company and took out $5,000 worth of spots. My deal was that I got 15 percent of the advertising revenue I sold, so this was a big deal to me.

So I worked up the spots and KVOO ran 'em. The only problem was, when we billed my old friend, he decided not to pony up the money. Since I'd taken my money up front, I had to dig in my pocket and come up with $750 of my own cash to pay the station back.

Thankfully, that kind of thing didn't happen too often.

Most all of the advertisers I've had a relationship with have been Tulsa-based. One of 'em, though, used me as the face of their national advertising. It was a company that made a little device called the E-Z Chord.

In case you've never seen one, an E-Z Chord is a device you put on the neck of your guitar, and instead of making chords with your fingers, you push buttons and the E-Z Chord does the job, with different numbers corresponding to different chords. It's an easy way to start playing the guitar immediately; just hook it up, and there you go. I can vouch for it. I've used it myself.

I can't remember the name of the man who had the E-Z Chord company, but I do remember that he was from McAlester, Oklahoma, where I'd spent some of my younger days. I never knew him then, though. It was just a coincidence. He contacted me sometime after I went to days at KVOO and hired me to be the E-Z Chord spokesman. I cut several TV spots for him, and I remember going to a TV studio in San Diego later, in the spring of '93, and cutting an E-Z Chord infomercial. By that time, It had been for sale for years, and it must've still been doing pretty well for him to be able to finance and buy the TV time for that infomercial I did.

His wife divorced him not long after that, and I'd always thought that was the end of the company. But John Wooley told me that he saw a Christmas catalog a year or two ago that had E-Z Chords for sale—and there was a picture of me with one on my guitar right beside the ordering information. So then I went to the Internet and found out, sure enough, that there are still lots of places where you can buy an E-Z Chord.

I'm not getting any more money out of 'em. I hope someone is.

※

In addition to John and Brett, my old buddy and former KVOO jock Wayne McCombs did a lot of digging and research to help jog my old memory. It was Wayne who came up with a clipping from the May 30, 1979 *Tulsa World* about "the first annual Billy Parker Celebrity Golf Classic." Wooley, who joined the *World* entertainment staff a few years later, says that one of the things he was told never to do at the paper was call anything a "first annual." As far as the *World* was concerned, no event became "annual" until it had been around a couple of years.

Somehow, though, we snuck through, because those were the first words in the *World* announcement of the tournament. And the Billy Parker Golf Classic did become an annual thing until, I believe, 1985, raising money first for the old Doctors' Hospital over on 41st Street and then for the Akdar Temple Crippled Children's

Transportation Fund, which helped provide transportation for kids who needed orthopedic or burn treatments at a Shriner's hospital. As a member of the Akdar Shrine myself, that charity was especially close to my heart.

A few days later, the *World* published a photo with Alla Mae Moss, Doctors' Hospital director of volunteers; Janey Woolley (no kin to my co-writer), director of nursing; and me, standing in front with a golf club and a big grin, looking like what they call in the golf world a "duffer." Wayne McCombs told my co-writers I wasn't too bad of a golfer, and while Wayne's right on most things, I don't think he's right on this one. I don't remember being very good at all, and my stance in that picture doesn't exactly look like Arnold Palmer's.

The "first annual" Billy Parker Golf Classic got underway on June 19, a Tuesday. About 200 golfers made it onto the links at Indian Springs Country Club in Broken Arrow, including area celebrities like Barry Switzer, then the head football coach at the University of Oklahoma, and his counterpart at Oklahoma State University, Jimmy Johnson. Well-known Tulsa TV guys like Lee Woodward and Jack Morris got in there as well.

It must've done all right. In one of the program books for the 1981 tournament, I've got an open letter that says the tournament provided "nursing education funds of almost $20,000" in its first two years.

At this late date, I can't tell you exactly how the event came about. The 1979 *World* story indicates that people from the hospital came to me, and since KVOO and the Stuart family were real strong in their commitment to the community, I imagine they were all for it and encouraged it to happen. Although I wasn't a regular golfer, I know I was into it, too, because it was another way the station and I could help people.

In 1982, we moved the tournament to the Oaks Country Club for a couple of years, and then back to Indian Springs in 1985, which is the last year Wayne has any material for. By then, we were splitting the proceeds between the Shriners' Fund and the Lifeline program at Doctor's Hospital, which was a new thing that helped elderly and handicapped people.

The '85 version was particularly strong on well-known Oklahoma baseball players, with Warren Spahn, Allie Reynolds, Jim Brewer, Don Demeter, Dale Mitchell, Tom Sturdivant, and Joe Frazier coming aboard. Noel Lemon, the former general manager of the Tulsa Roughnecks pro soccer team, returned to defend his 1984 title. I even had some western-swing greats on the links in '85, including my longtime pal Leon McAuliffe and two other guys from the early days of Bob Wills and His Texas Playboys, Smokey Dacus and Joe Frank Ferguson. Plus, Hank Thompson, one of the all-time great country and swing performers, showed up.

There were a lot more celebrities who came out to play a little golf and help us raise money over the years, and while I can't list them all, I did appreciate every last one of 'em. One name I do have to include is one you've seen before in this book. From the beginning, my great pal and neighbor Don Plummer was the Billy Parker Golf Classic's tournament chairman, and a lot of the credit for everything has to go to him. I sure couldn't have done it without Don.

If the Billy Parker Golf Classic ended in 1985, then it dovetailed with the beginning of another sporting event that carried my name. Nineteen-eighty-five was the first year, I believe, that the Billy Parker Lucky 13 Fishing Tournament was held. Like the Billy Parker Golf Classic, it started out a charity event and stayed that way. We began it to raise money for the Muscular Dystrophy Association; at some point we had the American Lung Association's Asthma Camp as a beneficiary, too.

The twist on this tournament, which made it a little different, was that whatever team came in at 13th place, based on the weight of the fish they caught, won a brand-new boat.

We went along with the yearly tournament for about 15 years, and then the event turned into a fundraiser for the Wagoner Area Chamber of Commerce. A story, written by Shane Ferris and published in the October 19, 2014 *Wagoner County American-Tribune*, gives a good explanation of how that happened. Shane quotes a friend of mine, Cyrina Lang, who organized the event for the Chamber. Said Cyrina:

"I started this [tournament] as a fundraiser for the Chamber, but we called it the Buddy Bass because the Lucky 13 was Billy Parker's. So when I saw him one day, I was telling him we were doing this and he said, 'Well, you use the Lucky 13 anytime you want to. I'll give it to you.' So the Chamber has the Billy Parker Lucky 13. We use this as a fundraiser to bring in the big open national bass tournaments and anything else to bring in tourism to Wagoner."

As I remember, Cyrina would always invite me up to Fort Gibson Lake to help with things, and I was there when Mr. Farris wrote his piece in that 2014 story. He even quoted me:

"Billy Parker was at the event, using a megaphone to announce the results of the tournament as the contestants weighed in.

"'The Lucky 13 started many years ago with some good people that were good friends of mine,' Parker said. 'They asked me to use my name as the Billy Parker Lucky 13. They asked me if I could fish, and I said, "No." So that made it good because I couldn't enter the tournament. It's been going on for many, many years and then Cyrina Lang took it over here a few years ago and continue to use my name which is a pleasure, because I love fishermen. I love the folks, I love their families and the entire works.'"

And let me add for this book that I also love the fact that something I lent my name to 30 years ago kept on going, giving those fishermen another tournament to look forward to and making money for a good cause.

BILLY PARKER

I met Billy Parker in 1979 when he was was an award-winning disc jockey for KVOO radio in Tulsa. I thought he'd be a great spokesman for my company—and he was. Little did I know at the time that he would become not only the voice of our company, but also a great friend.

In 1980 Billy became the talent for our TV telethon sponsorships of western movies that we aired in both Tulsa and Oklahoma City. Billy and I traveled many miles together during that time. Those movie sponsorships were done live, and Billy was absolutely the best talent for those live spots.

Using both radio and TV, Billy was critical in helping our company build a brand in Oklahoma.

I think back to 1979 and realize how fortunate I was to have met Billy—as well as his wife, Jerri, and their two sons. Our customers today still ask (and talk) about Billy. For over 40 years now, Billy has been a very close friend, and a big reason for our success in Oklahoma.

Enjoy those retirement years, Billy. You earned every bit of it. I'm so glad that our paths crossed.

~ BILL HAYNES ~

Bill Haynes Co.
THE FIRST NAME IN SIDING AND WINDOWS

Billy Parker

1170 AM BIG COUNTRY 98.5 FM

One of my later publicity photos.
COURTESY OF THE BILL HAYNES COMPANY.

CHAPTER FOURTEEN

In 1978, when I started daytimes at KVOO, FM radio had been around for a long time. It wasn't really even new back when I'd started out my radio career, 20 years earlier. But by the late 1960s, FM was playing a lot bigger role in the whole scene, with rock 'n' roll stations leading the charge. With FM, you could broadcast music in stereo, and there wasn't as much static on FM as there was on AM, either. The signal was clearer and just better for playing music.

At the time I left the all-night beat, we were still the No. 1 country station in Tulsa by a good margin. And we were back and forth, No. 1 and No. 2 in the market, with another AM station, news-talk KRMG. It seems like it would always be us one quarter, and then KRMG the next, as each of us climbed over the other one for the top spot every time a new Arbitron ratings book came out.

But even though two AM's were king of the hill in Tulsa, we could feel the breath of the FM's on the backs of our necks. That was especially true of KVOO, a music broadcaster rather than a talk station like KRMG.

Bill Payne was a great Oklahoma radio guy. In the late '70s, he'd bought the soul-music station KKUL, changed the call letters to KTFX, and relaunched it with a country format. So KTFX was our main competition at the time for the country-music listeners. KTFX was an FM station, and so was another competitor for the country audience, KWEN, better known as K95FM, which came along in 1982. It had been one of those "beautiful music" stations back in the '70s, playing easy-listening pop songs, and it had also spent a few years as a Top 40 station before flipping to country.

Now, all of a sudden, there were two other big country-music stations in the Tulsa market, and they were both on the FM side of the dial. This coincided with a time when more and more AM stations were going to talk and news and switching their music programming to FM. Thankfully, that wouldn't happen to KVOO-AM for many more years, but it was clear that we needed to add an FM station to our lineup if we wanted to stay at the top of the heap.

It took a little time, but Mr. Stuart was able to get one. The station that would become KVOO-FM in 1988 had started out back in 1973 as KBJH, the initials standing for Billy James Hargis, a popular Tulsa TV and radio preacher at the time, who put it on the air. Later, it became KCFO, playing contemporary Christian music, and that was the format when Harold Stuart made the deal to get it.

I won't lie to you—K95FM, and to a lesser extent KTFX, or K-FOX, as it was called—had begun eating into our listenership. We all knew that FM was the coming deal, music-wise, and people were getting more and more used to hearing their favorite songs in that format. We weren't about to give up on KVOO-AM, but we couldn't ignore the FM listeners either.

I've said throughout this book that I don't remember perfectly a lot of the stuff that happened in my life and career 'way back when, but luckily I have Wooley and Bingham to help fill in the blanks for me. Other people, like Wayne McCombs, have come forward, too. For this section, about the beginning of KVOO-FM, all of us were really helped by Mike Wilson, a great disc jockey and program director—and a good guy, too—who was right there when all of it happened. He'd been at K95FM, and then in 1985 I hired him. When Wooley talked to him for this book, Mike remembered that I brought him over to KVOO as not only a deejay, but also to become an assistant program director and music director.

He did those jobs for about a year on KVOO, he said, while Mr. Stuart was getting the rights to our new FM station, and then went to the FM as program director.

I thought the FM was KVOO from the first. But Mike knew different.

"We kicked the station off as KUSO, US 98," he told Wooley. "John Hunt was our general manager then. The AM was still doing very well, so the thought was that we'd make the FM different and go after a younger audience. So it was separate from KVOO at the beginning, although it had the same format. I remember one of the things we did was hire the former mayor of Tulsa, Terry Young, to do the morning show with our disc jockey Bill Stewart. He'd read the news and things like that. It was called *B.S. and the Mayor*, and we got quite a bit of publicity out of it.

"Not long after we went on the air, though, we had an ice storm and the TV tower where we had our antenna fell, and we were knocked off the air. I remember flying to Dallas, renting a Ryder truck, and taking a new transmitter back to Tulsa, while our engineer was somewhere up in Indiana finding a new antenna. We were back up in less than two days, which was really fast, but it still hurt us to be off the air that long."

A few months later, John Hunt was gone and Ron Blue—who had given me the chance to be on KFMJ almost 30 years earlier—was onboard as the KVOO GM. That's when the station changed names from US 98 to Country 98, KVOO-FM.

Well before that change happened, Mike and I had been working on the programming of the new station. I like to say that we programmed it with the help of Burger Street, a drive-through hamburger place on 21st and Harvard that's still there today. We'd get in the car and order at the window, get our sacks with the burger and fries in 'em, go back to the station, and sit there and eat while we talked over our ideas. We went through a lot of ground beef and French-fried potatoes while we figured out what we ought to do.

Like Mike told Wooley, the idea was to make the two stations different. From the beginning, although some of the news people appeared on both the FM and AM, each one had different sets of disc jockeys. One of the things Mike and I did was decide that there should be less news on the FM. KVOO-AM had news twice an hour, so we figured the other station should only have a news segment *once* an hour.

We had a real good news department then. Alan Lambert was our news director, and Jack Campbell, one of the all-time greats, was in there, too. Jack had been a deejay 'way back when KVOO played pop music, and he'd tried to stay with it when the station went country, but he knew country wasn't his thing. (I remember him saying he lasted about a week as a country jock.) So he switched to news and did real well. The whole bunch of newspeople were top-notch, whether they were called on to do their thing once an hour on the FM or twice on the AM.

Mike remembered another difference between the two stations. Both would have a certain number of golden oldies, songs "gone from the charts but not from your hearts," as the old Top 40 saying goes, but the AM would go a lot farther back to get 'em than the FM. KVOO-AM might go clear back to the '50s or even the '30s and '40s, especially to get a Bob Wills record. Because it was going for a younger crowd, the FM would mostly run oldies that hadn't been off the charts more than a few years, or even a few months.

So, while they were both called KVOO after 1988, there were a lot of differences in the two stations. I'm grateful to my old partner Mike Wilson for reminding me just how different they were.

A couple of things happened around that time that I'd just as soon not go into, because when I talk about 'em it sounds like I'm tooting my own horn and saying I'm some sort of big deal. But Brett and Wooley tell me that me getting these awards was important and we need to have that info in the book. So before I tell you what they were, let me say once again that I know it was all because of KVOO, like most of the rest of what went on in my career. If I hadn't been lucky enough to have been on that station, none of this would've happened to me.

Both of these honors, or awards, or whatever you want to call 'em, happened in 1987. On April 22, the Oklahoma State Legislature named me "the Official Oklahoma Ambassador of Country and Western Music." (Like the old joke goes, it was for both kinds of music, country *and* western.) There was a big official document, with a lot of "wherases" in it; one of them said how "the entertainment offered by Billy Parker has brought great joy to thousands of persons throughout the world." That was nice even though I'm not sure it was entirely true. The other thing happened on June 5, when Tulsa mayor Dick Crawford gave me one of the first-ever "Key Tulsan" awards. This was during a big festival called "Celebrate Tulsa," and, according to a letter I got, was given to people from T-town "who have made nationally recognized contributions in their chosen profession."

Again, I'm not sure I deserved either of those honors, but it was nice of the folks to give 'em to me. Honestly, when something like that happens, whether I think I earned it or not, it can't help but make me feel good, even though I don't like talking about it. I suspect a lot of people feel the exact same way.

KVOO-FM didn't take long at all to become a big player in the market, and things hummed along real evenly for a couple of years with both the FM and AM. Then, in January of 1990, the KVOO brand got a new owner. It was Great Empire Broadcasting, out of Wichita, owned by the Mikes—Mike Lynch and Mike Oatman. These were guys who loved country music and western swing; Mike Lynch, you might remember, was the guy, along with his dad, who'd bought KFMJ from Fred Jones back in 1960 and owned it when I first went to work there a year or two later. I knew the Mikes wanted KVOO bad. They burned up the roads back and forth between Tulsa and Wichita, looking everything over, talking to the folks at the station, and negotiating with Mr. Stuart.

At that time, Harold Stuart was in his late sixties, and I suspect he may have been looking to get out from under some of his responsibilities and start easing into a retirement situation. Also, as I've said earlier, he wasn't a big country-music fan. Actually, he wasn't a country-music fan at all. Going country had been strictly a business decision for him, and I don't think he ever particularly warmed up to KVOO's style of music. That may have made it easier for him to sell.

It was a different story with the Mikes. They both loved country, and Mike Oatman even had a show back at KFDI in Wichita, where he was known as "Ol' Mike." Ol' Mike's son, Andy, was also a country deejay, and a good one, who was personal friends with a lot of the younger acts in the business. I remember he was especially close to Ray Benson of Asleep at the Wheel. As a younger guy who knew music, he was also keen on Americana music, stuff that wasn't necessarily on the country charts but had a good following, like Oklahoma's Red Dirt music. Andy also did a little singing, and he wasn't bad at that, either. He'd done a recording in Wichita of "Catfish Boogie," the old Tennessee Ernie Ford hit, and it was plenty good enough to play over the air, which I did on several occasions.

Once Great Empire acquired us, Andy came in to do morning drive at the FM, and he really knew what he was doing. He loved it, too. He used to say, with his big grin, that it was great to get paid for being silly on the radio.

He was paid for a lot more than that, though. After Great Empire took over, he also became program director for both the stations. By that time, I believe, Jay Jones, our longtime p.d., had retired.

Things didn't change that much when Great Empire came on board. Their people were sales-oriented, just like Mr. Stuart had been. They trusted me, and Andy and I got along great and didn't have any trouble working together. The same went for Mike DeMarco, the guy they brought in from their station KTTS in Springfield, Mo., to be KVOO's new general manager. As time went along, I did eventually stop being operations director, because they more or less were directing everything from Wichita, but we still all got along real well, and I continued with my show and keeping up with all my advertising clients. Great Empire wasn't one of those outfits that would come in and clean house after taking over a station; I don't think they fired very many people at all. Even Jack Cresse stayed on, until health issues forced him to step back.

Really, as I look back on it I can tell you that Great Empire was definitely not one of those cutthroat operations. Of course, that was a different time, too. We were still in the good old days of radio, when things were a little more laid-back.

BILLY PARKER

Over the years, I've done an awful lot of interviews. A lot of them weren't even planned—they just had the opportunity to happen, and I rolled with 'em. I think the best example of that was when Charlton Heston showed up at the station one day, and they called back and told me he was there and would like to go on the air with me. I had no idea he was coming, but I welcomed him back and we had a good talk. A *big* guy, physically, but very nice.

To be honest, I got a little nervous any time anyone came to the studio for an interview. But I want to tell you now about the *most* anxious I ever got. I've talked throughout this book about Harold Stuart, who owned KVOO before Great Empire got it, but I want to impress upon you not only what a fine man Harold was, but also what a big figure he was on the national scene. He was real well known around Tulsa, of course, as a businessman and an attorney, but he was a lot of other things as well: a judge, a World War II hero, and the assistant secretary of the Navy under President Truman, just to name three. He had a lot of connections around the country and the world, a lot of famous friends. And even though he no longer owned KVOO in 1991, he got one of those celebrities to come by the station and do an interview with me, which was a big enough deal to be broadcast on both the AM and the FM.

Remember back at the first of the book, when I talked about growing up in north Tulsa and going to the Pines Theater to see movies—especially the singing-cowboy pictures, which were the ones I loved the best? Well, nearly fifty years after those days of my youth, I got to have a conversation with the greatest singing cowboy of them all, Gene Autry, who was coming through to be inducted into the Oklahoma Hall of Fame. It was only natural for him to come by KVOO; years before he got famous, he had appeared regularly on the station.

It was on November 15, 1991 when Harold Stuart brought him by for the interview, and I don't think I've ever had so many people sitting in on a radio interview in my life. Mr. Stuart was there, along with Will Rogers's son Jim. Johnny Western had come down, all the way from KFDI in Wichita; he'd known Gene in years gone by. John Wooley was there to record the event for the *Tulsa World*. Mr. Stuart was standing right behind me, whispering questions in my ear. And other deejays, newscasters, and sales people all found reasons to make their way into the studio. I didn't say anything to anyone then, but having an audience all around me, watching and listening every time I opened my mouth to ask Mr. Autry something, of course added more stress to the situation.

Somehow, though, I got through it all right. Mr. Autry was great, talking about everything from meeting Will Rogers in the train depot in Chelsea (Wooley's hometown) to the chances his major-league baseball team, the California Angels, had in the coming season. He was 84 years old at the time, and while he came in with a wooden cane, he never seemed to need it. I remember after the interview was over, I played his "Rudolph, the Red-Nosed Reindeer" over the air, and he signed autographs and posed for photos until everybody was satisfied. Wooley told me Mr. Autry asked for a copy of the story he was doing for the *World*, so I guess he enjoyed the experience.

I know *I* did, even though it made me awful nervous to be face-to-face, on the air, with the guy I'd loved so much when I was a kid. I kept it together, I think, while the interview was going on, but I let a little bit of my awe at the whole situation leak through after it was over, when I told Wooley, "If I never do another interview, I feel like my life has been fulfilled."

Of course, he quoted me for the end of his *World* story.

Since I'm talking about one of my co-writers, I figure this might be a good time to work in the story of a show John and I did together for many years on KVOO. I was especially proud to do it because of the tradition of KVOO and its importance to western-swing music. I've said before that my own career always goes back to KVOO; in the same way, if it hadn't been for KVOO broadcasting Bob Wills and His Texas Playboys—and later, Johnnie Lee Wills and His Boys—from the very beginning, I really don't believe that western swing would've made as big of an impact. It took a powerful station like KVOO to get the music out there to a lot of the country, and I'm convinced that the station played a huge part in making that kind of music popular, dating back to Bob's very first KVOO show in February '34.

Neither Wooley nor I know exactly when the *Wooley Wednesday* show started. Our best guess is 1991 or very early '92. I know that I'd done a new gospel album, *I'll Speak Out for You, Jesus*, that was released in January of '92, and that *Wooley Wednesday* started one day when John came up to interview me—so maybe that day, somewhere in the middle of January, was when it all began. Whether it was then or another day, I know that it was a time when he came up to see me before my show, and after the interview was done I invited him into the studio to go on the air with me.

Truth to tell, I blindsided him a little bit. We were pals, and I knew how much he loved western swing, so I pulled a lot of swing songs from Bob and Johnnie Lee and some others, and we talked about the artists and their music. Then, at one point—right over the air—I said, "Folks, if you'd like to hear us do a show like this once a week, give me a call."

In around five minutes, we'd logged 80 calls, with lots more coming in.

And that's how *Wooley Wednesday* was born.

Although later on we recorded it and put the recording over the air, we were live for years. Wooley would come in and we'd do it from 10 a.m. until noon—my regular slot on KVOO-AM—every Wednesday. Somewhere after we got started, the station started repeating it from 10 p.m. until midnight, also on Wednesdays, to take advantage of KVOO's expanded nighttime broadcast pattern.

Over the next several years, we were fortunate to have some great guests from the western swing realm come in and do the show with us. Sadly, the three biggest swing bandleaders from Tulsa—Bob Wills, Johnnie Lee Wills, and Leon McAuliffe—had passed by then. But we had Luke Wills, Bob and Johnnie Lee's bandleading brother, on the show, as well as lots of Wills sidemen like Clarence Cagle, Curly Lewis, Jimmie Widener, Don Tolle, and Glenn "Blub" Rhees. Maybe the biggest interview we had came along in

1996, when Bob's guitarist and arranger Eldon Shamblin, the man *Rolling Stone* magazine called the world's best rhythm guitar player, came up with his producer, Don Rhodes, to celebrate his 80th birthday and officially kick off the release of the album *There'll Be Some Changes Made*—which ended up being the last one he recorded.

O.W. Mayo, the longtime business manager for Bob and Johnnie Lee, was in his nineties then, and he was one of our most faithful listeners. In fact, he liked the show so much that he wrote a poem about it and gave us each a signed copy. Here's how it went:

> Wooley Wednesday what a radio show
> with John and Billy on KVOO
> You can hear your favorite artist
> as they play and sing
> They will make you pat your foot
> as they play that western swing.

And one time the great Roy Clark, listening as he started out from his Tulsa home on his way to the Roy Clark Celebrity Theatre in Branson, Mo., changed course, pulled into the KVOO parking lot, and did the rest of the show with Wooley and me.

We found out that people were passing tapes of the show around down in Nashville, and current country stars like Tracy Byrd, Steve Wariner, and Wade Hayes, who all loved swing, were digging *Wooley Wednesday* as well. There was talk about syndicating the show, but the people who were doing the talking were never quite able to pull the trigger.

THANKS—THANKS A LOT

Like I said, *Wooley Wednesday* was live, so occasionally things could suddenly go south without any warning. John reminded me the other day about a man who'd called in asking if we could play Marty Robbins' "My Woman, My Woman, My Wife" for his spouse on their anniversary. (We'd play some classic country as well as swing on the show.) I found Marty's greatest-hits album, cued up the track—and found out I'd missed it by one. Instead of "My Woman, My Woman, My Wife," the heartfelt dedication was followed by Marty's "Devil Woman."

The one John and I still laugh about the most, though, had to do with Glenn "Blub" Rhees, a guy I mentioned earlier. Blub had played saxophone in the bands of Bob, Johnnie Lee, and Luke—and in lots of other groups, too—and he was a real character.

Every year, around Bob's March 6 birthday, the Cain's Ballroom in Tulsa celebrated western swing with a weekend show and dance. At this time there were still quite a few people around who'd played with Bob and Johnnie Lee during their glory days at the Cain's, and they'd take that stage again for the big birthday bash. It was a big deal for fans from all over, and even if they weren't hired to play, a lot of the old musicians would show up at the Cain's for the shows.

Blub was one of 'em. But this particular year he'd had some health problems and no one was sure if he was going to make it. Then, one morning while Wooley and I were doing the show, he called up and asked if we could put him on the air so he could talk to the folks. Of course we did, and he said, "I just wanted everyone to know that I've been in the hospital, but I'm a lot better now and I'm planning on getting out and playing at the Bob Wills birthday deal."

John and I told him that was great and we were sorry he'd been sick.

"Oh, yeah," he said, still on the air. "I was *real* sick. Why, I had diarrhea for nine days!"

There were no tape delays, so his description of his internal (or is that external?) troubles went out to every single soul who'd tuned in. Wooley and I had a terrible time keeping ourselves from laughing out loud, and we didn't completely succeed.

The next thing up after Blub's call was a live spot for Roy & Candy's Music. Roy Ferguson, my old pal and musical partner, would call in every day and talk about specials at his store. This time, however, when I put him on the air the first thing he said was, "Kindly sounds like ol' Blub needs some *cheese*, don't it?"

Wooley and I just about lost it all, then. We were having such trouble keeping it together, in fact, that a member of Blub's family called up and got onto us for making light of his illness.

Back in the early '90s, Wooley wrote a music documentary called *Still Swingin'*, which had a little segment of us doing our show along with interviews from a lot of the old Texas Playboys as well as Tracy Byrd, the western-swing lover who was really taking off in country music about then; Stonehorse; and Asleep at the Wheel, among others. Andy O. had a bit in the movie as well, and Red Steagall made a great narrator. *Still Swingin'* included footage of the bands playing live shows, and while Wooley thought he'd made everything clear about the project, the Wheel's Ray Benson came up with ideas to the contrary. Once it came out, there was a real dustup between Wooley and Benson (although, I have to say, everybody else in the documentary, including Tracy Byrd, had no problems with their participation.)

The reason I mention this is because of something that happened while we were doing *Wooley Wednesday*, just after *Still Swingin*'s release on home video. John and I were in the studio when Opal Bledsoe came in with a FedEx package for him, telling him it had come C.O.D. from Asleep at the Wheel and she needed 15 bucks or something like that from him to cover the charges. Opal had been the bookkeeper for Harold Stuart and KVOO for years, and she was always such a good person. But she could seem a little bit severe if you didn't know her—and Wooley really hadn't been around her a lot.

So John opened up the envelope, and the biggest bunch of crap you've ever seen spilled out. I especially remember this cheesy strip of paper. Someone had written "BACKSTAGE PASS" with an ink pen and then laminated it and strung a piece of white twine through it.

He's looking at this, and trying to do the show, and every time we went to a record, Opal would ask him, sternly, "Well, what do you want to do about this?" I recall that he went to his wallet and didn't have enough money on him. I also believe that Ray Bingham and maybe Brett were in the studio at the time, and none of us offered to help him out.

We let him suffer and stay confused for quite a little bit before one of us broke down and started laughing. As it turned out, Ray and Brett had dummied up the envelope to make it look like a real collect FedEx package, stuffed it with photos and biographies and the fake backstage pass, and had Opal bring it in as a practical joke.

As I remember it, Wooley didn't seem to find it all that funny. But the rest of us did—including Opal, even though she never cracked a smile the whole time she was in the studio. She really sold it.

Wooley Wednesday ran for several years on KVOO-AM, always in that same time slot.

Then, in late 1999, we stopped doing it live and started recording, with a great engineer and producer, my buddy Dennis McAtee. It would run on Saturday mornings from seven until nine, and then again on Sunday nights. Since we weren't on Wednesdays anymore we changed the name of the show to *Still Swingin'*. We still got good Arbitron ratings; a lot of times, we'd be first or second in the market during those time periods.

The show kept going for almost 10 years and through another ownership change before finally being done in by a consultant who told John that his playlists were too "esoteric," a five-dollar word that meant they weren't the same old songs everyone else was playing. Wooley packed up and left, eventually starting his own public-radio western-swing show, *Swing on This*, that's still going today. Dennis and I kept on doing a show in the *Still Swingin'* time slot, changing the title to *Country Junction* and featuring more classic country music mixed in with the swing. I'm happy to say that Wooley joined me for that show several times, and he's had me on his as well.

John and I still have a lot of fun every time we get together, whether it's on the air or not. We've had fun with Brett, too, doing this book. I hope it shows.

In 1988, something happened to me record-wise that hadn't ever happened before. I had two Top 10 hits, "You Are My Angel," which sounded a little like an old rock 'n' roll ballad from the '50s, and "She's Sittin' Pretty." Both of them were from my *Always Country* album, which the General, Bart Barton, had released on his then-new label, Canyon Creek Records.

I should tell you that the chart they went Top 10 on was for *Canadian* country music. Yep, I was a hit in Canada, at least for a short time. Here in the States, the two singles showed up on the *Billboard* country chart, too, but nowhere close to the rankings they had in Canada.

I don't know. Maybe I should've done a little touring up north on the strength of those tunes. But KVOO was keeping me plenty busy, and I'm not sure whether there were any real offers anyway. For sure, though, I was glad to see the songs make a little noise, even if it *was* across the border.

As was usually the case with the General, we cut the tracks for *Always Country* down at his home base of Dallas. I was especially proud of a couple of tracks on the disc, "Thanks, E.T., Thanks A Lot," a tribute to my old bossman Ernest, and "Lord, If I Make It To

Heaven," my signature song. It was my first album in five years, and I think it came off pretty well.

I guess the General did, too, because a few years later he came to me with the idea of me doing a gospel album for Canyon Creek. He sent me up some songs he had, including one called "Bring Jesus Back to School," and that's how the album *I'll Speak Out for You, Jesus* got started. It was the first single off the record, and the only one that could've been thought of as political. The Supreme Court had put an end to public-school-sponsored prayer and Bible reading 'way back in the early '60s, but it was an issue that kept cropping up with different groups again and again. As you probably figured from the title, the song was all for getting rid of the restriction on prayer in school.

Funny enough, I was really kind of in the middle on that issue. I believed then, and I believe now, that you can pray anytime—at your desk, in your car, in the kitchen, wherever you happen to be. And if you're a kid in a class, you can always close your eyes for a minute and say what you've got to say to God. I knew that the song might be a little controversial, and I didn't want to make anyone mad, but pretty much all the feedback I got was favorable. To me, it was bigger than some political issue of the right versus the left. It was more about values. That's really why I wanted to do the album. I think every country artist from my era felt the same way; just about all of us were raised to believe in God and Jesus, and a lot of us had a deeper religious background. I was one of 'em. You may remember me telling you in the first part of this book about my mom playing piano in church, and how as a youngster I even tried a little bit of preaching to the kids back there in north Tulsa.

THANKS—THANKS A LOT

Jerri was raised the same way. After we were married, her mother, Ruby Hamblin, would come out occasionally to places where I was playing, and in those days I liked to end my show with a religious number—just like I used to do with what I called the "Song of Inspiration" on my radio broadcasts. A lot of times I'd close a show with "Just A Closer Walk with Thee." And pretty much all my mother-in-law would ever say was that she really liked that gospel number at the end.

Of course, I wanted *I'll Speak Out for You, Jesus* to do good saleswise, and I think it did all right. Because of it, the International Country Gospel Music Association gave me its Top Country Personality award in '93. That was probably the most unexpected award I ever got, but it was also one of the ones I was proudest of. I have to tell you, though, it didn't happen because the General called me up and said, "Hey, Billy, let's do a gospel album because we know how to market it and it'll make a lot of money." I did it because I believe in God and the church and I loved having the opportunity to sing about those things. I think, really, that I wanted to do it for self's sake more than for any other reason.

Once again, "Lord, If I Make It to Heaven" was included on an album of mine. The *I'll Speak Out for You, Jesus* track was the same one we had on *Always Country*, which was also the one that had been released by Sunshine Country as a single. There were a couple of reasons the song showed up so many times on my albums. First of all, Bart Barton had produced it down in Nashville, so it was his master and he could use it wherever he wanted. Second, it had done good on the charts as a single and I always played it when

I did a live show. At that time, Ray Bingham was booking me a lot, so the song was familiar to a lot of people around the area. So there was a little bit of a recognition factor there.

I sure didn't mind. I've always thought of it as Jerri's song and anytime I could have it on an album or sing it in person, I was happy to do it.

⭐

Years ago, someone told me he really wanted to visit the schoolhouse in Texas where Bob Wills went as a kid. He said he figured it had to be the biggest building in the world to have enough room for all the people who said they went to school with Bob.

It's kind of the same thing when it comes to being in Bob's Texas Playboys. I'll bet I've had hundreds of people come up to me and tell me that they played with Bob, or their dad or uncle or somebody else in their family was in Bob's band. A lot of times there's some truth to that, because Bob disbanded his Texas Playboys in the early '60s but kept on touring, bringing only one or maybe two other musicians on the road with him. He and his one or two sidemen would play with house bands, or with bands on package tours, and a lot of those people who played with Bob were in house bands or touring bands that backed him once, or even several times.

Our friend Curly Lewis, who spent some time fiddling and singing in Bob's band and even more time in Johnnie Lee's, used to say that if you rode the bus with or got a check from a bandleader, then you could say you were a member of his band.

I can't say I was a Texas Playboy, and I never *have* said it, even though I've said—in this book—that I played four or five dates with Bob when I was with Ernest. We were on one of those touring shows that featured several different artists, and the Texas Troubadours were the backing band for all the featured performers. I got to play behind Bob and even visit with him a little bit, but that was the extent of it. It was after he'd had his first stroke, and I remember him talking pretty slow, but it was an honor just to be able to visit a little and work on the same stage with him.

Johnnie Lee is a little bit of a different story. Since he stayed in the Tulsa area, I played a lot with him over the years, especially after he let his band go and used my buddy Roy Ferguson's band, the Royals, whenever he had an engagement. I can truthfully say we were good pals.

The point of all this is that I really thought a lot of Bob and Johnnie Lee, and I loved their music, which Bob had popularized and Johnnie Lee had carried on, both using Tulsa's Cain's Ballroom as their base. So when my old friend Russell Sims, who'd produced and released some of my earlier records—and several for Johnnie Lee, too—talked to me about doing a western-swing album, I was all for it.

This would've probably been in early 1996, and at the time, Russell and I had been going back and forth about doing a record for quite a while. He was still down in Nashville, and he'd call up and say, "Anytime you want to do a session, you let me know and we'll get it done."

What got my attention this time was him saying that I could have Tommy Allsup as the music director for the album. Tommy was a good friend, another Okie, who'd done great in the music business. Fans in the pop realm knew him as the guy who'd lost a coin toss to Ritchie Valens back in February of '59, so that Valens had gotten Tommy's seat on the private plane that crashed and killed him, Buddy Holly, and the Big Bopper. Western-swing fans knew that Tommy had worked in Johnnie Lee's band and produced several records for Bob, including the famous *For the Last Time* set of records. He'd done a lot of production and session work on all kinds of different records, but he was very well-known to western-swing fans, and he knew what we were doing on *Wooley Wednesday*.

So with that in mind, Russell and I worked out what songs we were going to do, more or less over the phone. I wanted to do mostly the top Bob Wills songs, the ones everyone had heard and the ones I especially liked. Russell had his input as well.

In his files on me and *Wooley Wednesday*, John has a sheet in my handwriting with a preliminary list of the songs I wanted to record for the album that ended up with the title *Swingin' with Bob*. Three of those didn't make the album. Two weren't actually Bob Wills tunes. "Bob, All the Playboys, and Me" was a Charlie Williams composition recorded by Dorsey Burnette back in '74, and "Oakie Boogie," had been written by western-swinger Johnny Tyler and made into a big hit in 1947 by Woody Guthrie's cousin Jack Guthrie, another Oklahoman. (In doing their research, my co-writers came up with this: The same year "Oakie Boogie" was a hit, Jack Guthrie sang it in a film called *Hollywood Barn Dance*. It was Guthrie's only appearance in the movies—and the film starred my old boss, Ernest Tubb.) The only Wills song I originally chose that got left off was "Blues for Dixie," which Mr. Mayo had written (with some uncredited help from Cindy Walker.)

Instead of those, we added "Take Me Back to Tulsa," "San Antonio Rose," and "I Knew the Moment I Lost You," three of Bob's biggest numbers. They fit in well with the other seven tunes we'd chosen, all hits like "Maiden's Prayer," "Roly Poly," and "Time Changes Everything."

The sessions went off great, with Russell Sims producing, Tommy as the music director and rhythm guitarist, and top Nashville pickers like piano player Pig Robbins, fiddler Buddy Spicher, and guitarist Pete Wade joining with Bob Wills's great steel guitarist Bobby Koefer in the studio. For backup vocals, I had Darrell McCall, a star himself, who'd been on several of my records, including "(Who's Gonna Sing) The Last Country Song." Wooley wrote the liner notes, and Russell released it on his own label, Sims Records.

I'm still real proud of that album, although I've got to say I still would've liked to have had Mr. Mayo's number on there. It would've been too late for him to hear it, though, as he'd passed on a couple of years earlier at the age of 93. In big part because of Mr. Mayo, we'd played the fire out of another version of "Blues for Dixie" on *Wooley Wednesday* a few years before. It was the one Lyle Lovett recorded with Asleep at the Wheel for the Wheel's first all-Bob Wills album, *Tribute to the Music of Bob Wills and the Texas Playboys*. It had come out in '93, just a few months before Mr. Mayo died, and because we played it so much, our good friend went to his grave thinking he had a big radio hit.

BILLY PARKER

Billy Parker is one of the best guys I have ever known and worked with. He is a very special person with a big heart for family, friends and strangers. He has helped countless artists over the years by stepping up and out early on their music, and he taught me to do the same.

Most of the performers Billy knows would do anything for him—shows, interviews, special radio promotions. He was always a stand-up guy, and, whether he was dealing with his radio staff or advertising clients, one of the hardest-working people I have ever seen.

I worked a little over four years with Billy Parker, and I wouldn't trade that time for anything. I'm happy to say we remain close friends today. Congratulations, Billy, on your new book and your great hall of fame career!

~ **MIKE WILSON** ~

Me with Roy Clark and co-author John Wooley during a *Wooley Wednesday* broadcast.

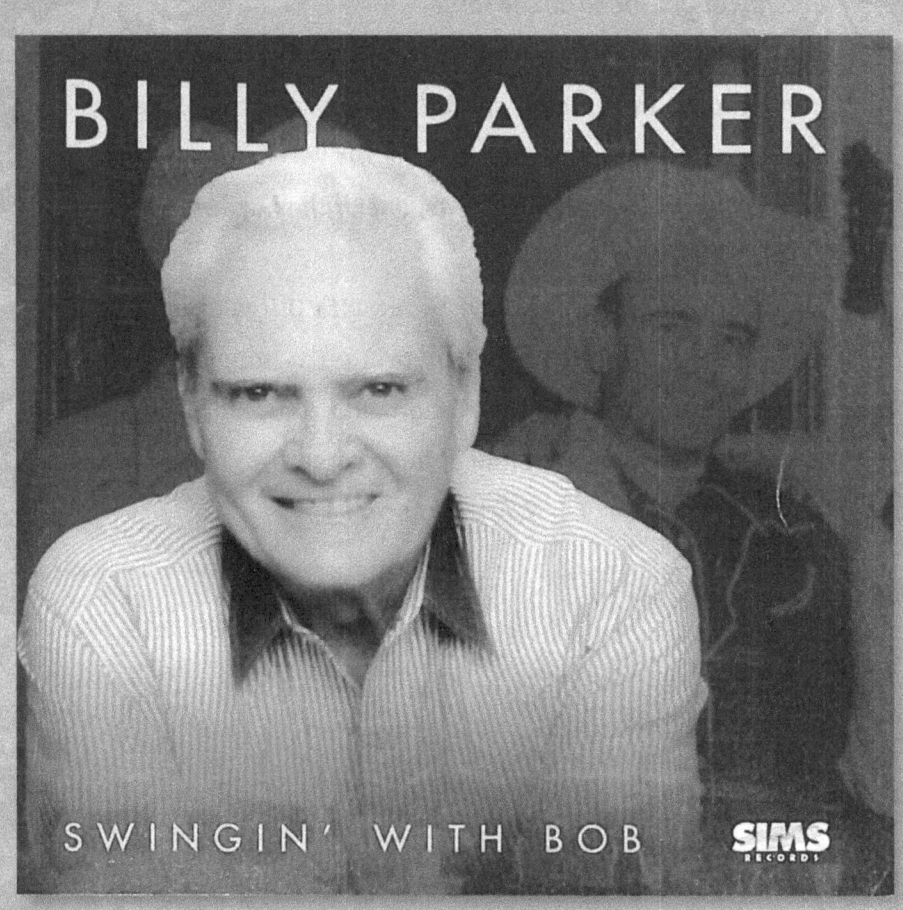

The CD cover to my *Swingin' with Bob* tribute CD to the great Bob Wills.

CHAPTER FIFTEEN

It's kind of a funny coincidence that two other big things happened to me in each of the years my final two albums got released. In 1992, when *I'll Speak Out for You, Jesus* came out, I had the honor of being elected to the Country Music Disc Jockey Hall of Fame in Nashville. And in 1996, the year Russell Sims put out *Swingin' with Bob* on Sims Records, I got to celebrate my 25th anniversary with KVOO.

I remember being down at the Opryland Hotel when they gave me the deejay award. It was during the Saturday night banquet at the Country Radio Seminar in Nashville, which always brings in people from all over.

When I got back, Wooley called me up to do a story for the *Tulsa World* about it, and I told him I'd been more nervous about it than I'd been about anything in my life.

He quoted me in his story, which ran in the March 11th *World*: "It was a big crowd, all your peers are there, all the radio people that I look up to. For me to receive the award—well, it really bumfuzzled me. I didn't feel as much deserving of it as I felt great—just great inside."

At that time, and I don't think it's changed, they inducted one living and one deceased deejay each year. Since I was in the first category, I had to give an acceptance speech. I don't remember much about it except for thanking Jack Cresse for bringing me to KVOO; Harold Stuart and his son, Jon, the former owners, for all they did for me and my career; and the station's general manager at the time, Mike DeMarco, for letting me carry on the real country-music tradition. I also remember that I got a standing ovation from the crowd, which was another surprise.

I've heard it's a sign of not being quite right when you start quoting your own self, but I liked my words that Wooley closed the story with, after telling his readers I thought this award topped every other one I'd gotten. Here they are:

"This is the ultimate. I didn't really know what it meant until I was nominated for it. But this is the Hall of Fame award for radio and television—that's the way the plaque reads—and that would've really been my last wish in the business, to be inducted into the Disc Jockey Hall of Fame."

I remember when Hank Thompson got inducted into the Country Music Hall of Fame, back in 1989. He said, "Does this mean it's over? Is it time to get out?"

Well, it sure wasn't for him. And it wasn't for me, either.

The year after the Disc Jockey Hall of Fame thing, I got inducted into the Western Swing Hall of Fame in Sacramento, California. (The same year, Gilly Travel in Tulsa sponsored a "Billy Parker Celebration Cruise" to Alaska that Jerri and I hosted.) Then, in 1995, the Oklahoma Association of Broadcasters gave me its Lifetime Achievement Award. I didn't have to go quite as far to get that one as I did the other two; it was presented to me during a dinner at Fountainhead Resort at Lake Eufaula, about an hour and a half from our house. I'd known Carl C. Smith, the executive director at OAB, for about 30 years at that point in our lives. He'd been in management at KFMJ when I first got on as a deejay there. In fact, he'd been at the station when I'd left to go with Ernest.

It was another great honor. I thought then, and I still think now, that there were many more people around who deserved to get it before I did. But I won't lie—I was thrilled to death when they gave it to me.

Meanwhile, like Hank Thompson, I kept right on working, pickin' and grinnin', doing my 10 a.m. 'til noon show every weekday—including *Wooley Wednesday* and a new one I'd come up with, *Country Gold Thursday*—and keeping up with all of my sales responsibilities. I stayed plenty busy, ratings were good, and everybody was getting along well. In '96, as I said earlier, the Mikes and Great Empire did a real nice thing, recognizing the fact that I'd been with KVOO (on the AM side) for 25 straight years. We got a lot of publicity about it, and Mike DeMarco went on the record with Wooley and the *Tulsa World* to say that he really hadn't known how "far-reaching" my reputation was until he and I took a couple of trips to Nashville together. In a story the paper ran on August 1, 1996, DeMarco said it was only then that he "saw how many people in the industry—including big stars—recognized him [that'd be me] on sight, and went out of their way to stop and speak to him. I knew he was a well-known broadcaster; I didn't know the extent of his fame in country music."

Talk about making you feel good. I'm not so sure I was as well-known in Nashville as Mike made me out to be, but I *had* been in the business for a long time and had gotten acquainted with a whole lot of artists along the way. More important, I think, was that they were *country-music* people, and they just tended to be kinder and more considerate than the stars you might find in other areas. That's *my* feeling, anyway.

Things at the radio station went along fine for a couple more years, as least as far as I was concerned. In 1998, the Oklahoma Association of Broadcasters decided to give me another award. This time, I got put in the OAB Hall of Fame. Two of us went in that year. The other was Bob Brown, a great guy who had a basket full of Emmys for his work on ABC-TV's 20/20 news program. I'd known Bob since back around 1960, when he was just starting in radio and doing the engineering for Marvin McCullough's show on KRMG. (Remember Marvin? The guy responsible for me cutting "Thanks A Lot" 'way back when, playing it one time on his show—at the wrong speed?) It was real good to see Bob again. Just like with the OAB Lifetime Achievement Award, I thought there were a lot of other Okies who deserved the honor more than I did. But it sure made me proud when they gave it to me. I mean, it was from my peers, the people from my home state, and, as the old saying goes, home is where the heart is.

So everything was good as far as I was concerned. But since I wasn't in management any longer, I wasn't really privy to what was going on behind the scenes. When Harold and Jon Stuart owned the station, they'd have me in on board meetings, I'd even vote with them on different things. Then, I'd always be up to speed on what might be happening with the station. But when Great Empire came along, I wasn't involved too much in that area. Great Empire brought in its own people, which was fine with me. They were good folks and I had plenty to do without having to be in management.

I said all that to say that it was a little bit of a shock to me when I found out that Mike Oatman and Mike Lynch were wanting to sell—not just KVOO-AM and its sister stations in Tulsa, which now included a third country station called KCKI, but every one they had in every market—13 in all. I'm pretty sure they decided to put everything up for sale because they had started experiencing some real serious health problems. It was only a few years before both of them were gone. They even passed away in the same place, the M.D. Anderson Cancer Center in Houston. Mike Oatman died there in 2003, Mike Lynch in 2004. (Ol' Mike's son Andy Oatman passed away only 16 years after his dad—far too early.)

In the late '90s, Great Empire found its buyer, a big operation out of Milwaukee called the Journal Broadcast Group. As we were doing this book, we looked at a story in the *World*, written by business writer Shaun Schafer for the June 16, 1999 paper. It told us that Journal Broadcast had announced its plans to buy Great Empire back in August '98, and the company had been waiting for FCC approval ever since. Schaefer also gave the sizes of the two companies. Great Empire had around 275 people on its payroll, which seems plenty big to me. But Journal Communications, Journal Broadcast Group's parent company, employed more than 7,000, spread out over newspapers, other publishing, radio, and television.

In the story, Mike Oatman was quoted as saying, "We believe the communities in which we operate will welcome Journal and note little change in our style of operation."

We all know, though, that when a new outfit comes in and takes over, things do change—and this deal was sure no exception. Mike DeMarco stayed on as general manager, but Journal started bringing in a bunch of consultants and different people who, in my opinion, didn't really respect or have any knowledge of what I thought was *real* country music. I don't mean to say they were bad people. They just didn't know what the station had stood for all these years. (To be fair, they also stopped Andy Oatman from playing the Americana music he loved, too.)

A couple of months after Journal took over, after I'd done a lot of thinking and talking to Jerri on the subject, I told Mike DeMarco that I wanted to resign from my daily show. The idea was that John and I would continue to do a show with the *Wooley Wednesday* western-swing format, but we'd record it for playing on the weekends. That's when Dennis McAtee started working with us and we changed the name to *Still Swingin'*. Content-wise, it was the same two-hour show we'd been doing on Wednesday mornings, but now instead of going live we taped it during the week for airing Saturday morning and repeating on Sunday night.

Because I wasn't going to be on the air daily any longer, word leaked out that I was retiring—which wasn't true. I was still performing, and I was still working with all my advertising accounts on both radio and TV. I had plenty to do. But when a couple of the local TV stations announced I was hanging it up, I had to set the record straight. Once again, I went to the *Tulsa World*. But this time, since Wooley was a part of the story, Jim Vance wrote the article, which came out on November 14, 1999.

Here's what I told Jim:

"I've been in radio for 28 years. I've been in all kinds of positions at KVOO from DJ to operations manager, and I just thought it was time to move over and let those young consultants use that research they come up with to operate the station to its fullest and make it greater than ever."

I don't think you have to read between those lines too much to understand why I decided this was the time for me to step back a little bit. I know that Journal could've let me go right then. But after DeMarco and I talked, we agreed I would be, as I told Jim Vance, "a full-time employee who just doesn't have to go into the office every day." That was pretty much the truth. Over the years, I'd developed a lot of accounts, and many of them had become good friends. I believed in their products and was glad to keep being their spokesman and stay up with whatever they needed. Add *Still Swingin'* to that, and it was still just about a forty-hour-a-week job.

I'm not sure how long *Still Swingin'* lasted after that, but it was at least three years before the consultant Wooley always referred to as "Floyd the Barber's evil twin" caught him after one of our tapings, told him that people liked their music to be familiar, and said what he was putting on the *Still Swingin'* playlist wasn't *familiar* enough. John, who was still with the *Tulsa World* then, listened to what the man had to say and then told him, "I've already got a job" and went into the studio to clean out his western-swing albums and CDs. (I think he managed to pick up a few of mine, too. At least, I accuse him of that to this day.)

That was John's farewell to the Journal Broadcast Group, and the last day for *Still Swingin'*. Dennis and I continued in the same time slot with *Billy Parker's Country Junction*. There was still a little swing on each show, for sure, but, as I mentioned in the last chapter, it was a lot heavier on classic country, my all-time favorite kind of music. And while Wooley was officially off the payroll, he visited the show many times, and we always had a great time on the air, just as we'd had on *Wooley Wednesday*. We've stayed good friends to this day.

Country Junction would end up running for about a dozen more years, until I really *did* retire from the business.

On May 16, 2002, the *Tulsa World* ran an editorial cartoon by David Simpson that showed an angry mob in cowboy hats, with pitchforks and a noose, outside a building that had "TULSA'S KVOO RADIO" on its side. Underneath it were the words "NOW ALL-TALK, NO

MORE MUSIC." And from inside, a deejay is looking out, saying, "Good grief... It's Bob Wills and the Texas Playboys!"

For my money, that cartoon told you everything you needed to know about the Journal Broadcast Group's decision to change not only the format of KVOO-AM—which would've been bad enough—but also its call letters. Now, the station where I'd spent more than 30 years of my life, the one whose call letters had stood for Voice of Oklahoma since before I was born, was no longer broadcasting country music. It had become KFAQ, the kind of political-talk station that had become popular back then.

Truthfully, I knew that KVOO-AM had been on borrowed time. As I said earlier, the trend for many years had been to move music programming to FM outlets, leaving AM for talk, whether sports, news, politics, or a combination. KVOO-AM's biggest competitor in town, KRMG, was a news-talk station, and had been for years when KFAQ came along to try a similar format.

Still, it hurt to see it go. I know it hurt a lot of other people, too, listeners who'd grown up when there was only an AM KVOO. They realized something was going away that they could never get back. An old friend was riding off into the sunset. To them, and to me, it was a sad time.

My pal Bob O'Shea, a fine deejay who was then on the late shift at KVOO-AM, was one of those people. He was the one on the air just before midnight on May 15, 2002, when KVOO-AM died and KFAQ was born. Bob put some thought into the last three records he played; he knew what a big deal this was. The last song ever played on KVOO-AM was "Take Me Back to Tulsa," by Bob

Wills and His Texas Playboys. The second to last was "T-U-L-S-A Straight Ahead" by Asleep at the Wheel. And the third to last was one from my *(Who's Gonna Sing) The Last Country Song* disc, "Hello Out There." Although it's kind of a cheating song, where the singer is saying hello to someone who might be birddogging the singer's girlfriend, it was a good choice as far as I was concerned. After all, how many years of nights and days had I been saying "hello out there" to the folks who'd tuned in faithfully to KVOO-AM?

At first, Journal Broadcast Group wanted to have *Still Swingin'* run on both KVOO-FM and KFAQ. (Wooley and I were still doing the show when the switch from KVOO-AM came.) I think it worked that way for a while, but then, in 2003, Journal changed its other Tulsa country station to the country oldies format, and that's where we landed. KXBL, formerly known as KCKI, or KICK 99, had been in the country market since 1993, but this was the first time it had been dedicated completely to oldies.

"Oldies," though, meant something different to the station's management and consultants than it did to me. They might have hung that tag on records by people like Ronnie Milsap or the Bellamy Brothers, where I'd think more along the lines of Bill Anderson and Jeannie Seely and even farther back to stars like Hank Williams and Bob Wills. My playlists reflected what I thought oldies were, both on *Still Swingin'* and, after John left, *Country Junction*.

I have to say that, unlike Wooley, I didn't get didn't get much negative feedback from anyone involved in programming or managing the station. They all pretty much left me alone, although we started getting a lot of visitors in the studio on the days we taped. In some ways, it was just another way of helping people out, like I'd done on the overnight show and later on, when I was operations and music director. We'd have people coming in to plug events around the area, artists—both local and national—stopping by to talk a little bit about their new records, advertisers doing live bits with me about their products. Sometimes it got to where you couldn't stir 'em with a stick. I was glad that people still thought enough of me and what I did to want to be on my shows, so I welcomed them all and tried to take care of 'em the best I could.

Let me talk a minute here about my other collaborator on this book, Brett Bingham. You know he's the nephew of Ray Bingham, who managed me and booked me for so many years. (And if you're reading this, Ray, I wouldn't mind if you got out there and hustled me up another couple of gigs. I've kinda been waiting for the phone to ring.) In October of 2005, the folks at the Oklahoma Music Hall of Fame decided to induct me, and when word got out, Brett got hold of Ray and thought it would be a good idea if a special radio show was put together to celebrate my induction. They tried at first to keep it a secret from me, but since they were going to use my *Country Junction* time slot, they had to let me know about it.

Well, they sure did some kind of job. Andy Oatman and Brett were the hosts, and they had all kinds of people on it, from Roy Ferguson and Candy Noe to Hank Thompson, Red Steagall, Roy Clark, and Reba McEntire. Randy Bush, who was general manager of KVOO and KXBL, gave it the green light, and every time I think about it I'm proud and honored, not only because of all the artists who took their time to come on and say something about me, but also because of all the work that Brett and Ray and Andy put into it.

Because I don't want Wooley to feel left out, I ought to add that when I was officially put into the Oklahoma Music Hall of Fame down in Muskogee, John was the one who inducted me.

I grew up around deejays. My dad was one, his friends were deejays; I was always around country deejays. I knew the legend of Billy Parker, and when I had the opportunity to move to Tulsa and take this job I did—not knowing what to expect. I was a snot-nosed 27-year-old kid coming down to be the program director, which meant, technically speaking, I could have been saying, "Billy, you need to do this. Billy, you need to do that."

I didn't know what I was doing, I was lost, and instead of walking in the door and having him look at me as the snot-nosed kid who didn't know what was going on, he took me under his wing. He basically held my hand for the first 5 or 6 years while I got my feet under me at KVOO.

It was that, and the birthday cards he sends to my son every year, and the calls when somebody's sick—it's those type things that I'll always remember about Billy Parker. Beyond the fame, it's the kind of man that he is.

~ **ANDY OATMAN** ~

(from the 2005 Billy Parker radio tribute)

Like Andy, I've known a lot of disc jockeys over the years. Billy Parker is one of the few who is a true communicator. When you listen to him, he may be talking to thousands of people at once—but you feel like he's talking just to you. That's a very special trait. He's loved by everyone who knows him, and by thousands who don't.

~ **DENNIS MCATEE** ~
(from the 2005 Billy Parker radio tribute)

Dennis McAtee, Andy Oatman, and co-author Brett Bingham
PHOTO COURTESY OF *TULSA WORLD*.

CHAPTER SIXTEEN

People say that the older you get, the faster time goes, and that's sure the way it's happened with me. When I look back on it, my last 10 years of deejaying seems to have gone by in a flash. For all that time, I was still doing the two-hour weekend show and taking care of my clients, and on taping day the studio was usually full of people either wanting to be on the air or just happy to watch the proceedings. Once when Wooley came up, he said that doing a show with all the folks in the studio was like trying to have a prayer meeting in a wind tunnel. But I was glad people still wanted to be a part of my shows. We never had any trouble finding advertisers or sponsors, and, what's more, everyone in management left me alone to do my thing. I could talk to who I wanted, and I could play who I wanted.

Being left alone, now that I think about it, had a lot to do with why I stayed in the business as long as I did. In my nearly 45 years at KVOO, I went through a whole lot of managers and the station went through a whole lot of changes. But one thing I can say is that no one ever tried to change *me*. There may have been different policies about what you could or couldn't play on the air, and I imagine for my last several years I was the only one still playing Bob Wills and Ernest Tubb, as well as local artists. But in all my years with the KVOO family of stations, nobody told me what I could or couldn't play, going clear back to when I started with *The Big Rigger Show*.

I'm not real sure why I was allowed to call my own shots right up to the end. I think maybe they knew I was satisfying an audience, which was something I'd always tried to do. And I was still doing a good job of selling for the station, something that's important no matter *who's* in charge. And I think station management knew that I could never be something I wasn't, something fake. I couldn't fake it then, and I can't fake it now.

It may look like me leaving had something to do with another change in owners, since Scripps came along to merge with the Journal group in 2014, and I retired in 2015. But that's more of a coincidence than anything else. Here's the truth: I saw that more changes were coming—not just in Tulsa, but throughout the business. From conversations with people in the business and just keeping my eyes and ears open, I *detected* it. I knew big changes were on the way in country radio. A wave was coming, and you could either try to swim with it or let it crush you. That was my feeling, and I think I was right.

Sometimes, people leave a job they've had for years because a manager comes in that they don't like and starts riding them or making them do a lot of things different. That wasn't at all the case with me. In fact, over all the years I can't remember anybody trying to change me or what I did on the air. I don't recall ever having any problems or conflicts with a manager; in fact, some of my old managers and I still stay connected on the Internet. I got along with *everybody*—even though I sometimes had to work at it. But then again, nobody—except Jerri—has ever told me what to do. That was the way I liked it. I liked my freedom, and maybe I thought I'd earned it.

I can honestly say, too, that I wasn't asked to retire. Maybe they would've pulled the plug on me if I'd stayed longer, but I'll never know, and there sure weren't any indications they were unhappy. Everybody at the station was very good to me right up until my final show—and past it, really, because they threw an "Over and Out" party at the Cain's Ballroom for me on January 22, 2016, exactly a month after I'd taped the last of my programs. (It went out over the air on December 26 and 27, the last weekend of 2015.) They really did things up first-class, sending out invitations and everything, and more people showed up than I could have possibly imagined. It was real nice, and I was humbled and honored by all the folks who came out that evening, just to say hi or to share a story or two about my days in radio.

About eight months before that, even before I officially announced that I was retiring, Ray and Brett Bingham and John Wooley cooked up an event that the *Tulsa World*'s Jimmie Tramel thought might have been "the feel-good event of the year." That's what he wrote, anyway, in his story about *Thanks A Lot—the Billy Parker Tribute*," which the Binghams and Wooley produced. John and Brett hosted it, and, once again, I was amazed at the people who showed up or passed along good words: Dolly Parton sent a card that said, "We will always love you," and Marty Stuart, Claude Gray, and T.G. Sheppard wrote in, too. The Oak Ridge Boys sent a great big greeting card they called a "colossal-gram."

And then, there were the folks who came to Tulsa just for the event. I was so proud to have artists like Becky Hobbs, Leroy Van Dyke, Red Steagall, Peggy Rains, Deborah Allen, and Jana Jae perform, with the Tulsa Playboys on hand to back everyone up. Roy Clark and Buck Trent dropped by, and so did longtime deejay pals like Jack Fox and Andy Oatman. My good friends from Stonehorse, Mike and Brent Self, Donnie Talbert, and Darlene Passmore, came in to play. There was even someone there from the pop realm: Taylor Hanson, who's done so well in the rock-music business with his brothers. It was just a great event that I'll always remember.

Of course, the Binghams and Wooley knew that I was pretty close to wrapping up my radio career when they put *Thanks A Lot* together. I'd said to them just what I'm saying to you now—I knew it was time for me to leave. I didn't want to work under the changes I detected were coming. I wanted to go out with some respect, and I think I did.

When I taped my very last show, Jimmie Tramel—a great writer and good guy—came up to do a story, which ran on Christmas Day, 2015. I remember him asking me how I felt about all of this, about doing a final broadcast, about leaving the airwaves. I told him something that I think makes for a good ending to this chapter—of this book, and of my life.

"I don't want anybody to be sad," I told him. "But you know what? I hope they do miss me, because if they didn't miss me, I wasted a lot of years."

Of course, I was kidding with Jimmie. I'd never really think all those years I spent in the radio and music business were in any way wasted, if only because of the great people I met and knew and worked with along the way. I've mentioned a lot of them already, but I want to make sure to remember a few more right now.

A good place to start would be with Larry Scott, who was a true hall of famer. I guess he was best known for doing his *Interstate Road Show*, an overnight program, out of KWKH in Shreveport, Louisiana for years before coming to KVOO to do the same thing. (Of course, this was after the Big Rigger Show, when I'd moved to daytimes.) He had deejay of the year awards from both the CMA and the ACM, and he loved his country music and western swing.

Larry was a great guy, one of my very best friends in the business for many years. From the late '60s through the early '80s, before he started at KWKH, he'd worked stations in the L.A. area, and he was real good about playing my records on his shows, no matter where he was.

That brings up another thing I'd like to mention. I wrote earlier about some of the overnight guys, myself included, and how we were always trying to get our own records played at the same time we were doing our shows. I'm talking about people like Charlie Douglas out of WWL in New Orleans, Bill Mack on WBAP in Fort Worth, and Billy Cole at WHO in Des Moines, as well as Larry at KWKH. Since we were all competing with one another for a run on the country charts, you might think that we wouldn't have been too eager to plug each other.

Truthfully, though, I can tell you I don't think we ever felt that kind of competitiveness. In fact, we would play one another's records and even talk about any gigs the other guys might be playing around our broadcast area. If I was coming to play in or near Fort Worth, for instance, Bill Mack would let his listeners know when I was coming and give them all the info about the date. He might even do a call-in with me. And I'd do the same thing for any one of them. We may have been in competition as broadcasters and recording artists, but that didn't mean we wouldn't help each other out.

It wasn't just the national broadcasters, either. During a long stretch of my time at KVOO, it was either us or the news-talk station KRMG, both 50,000-watt powerhouses, that would be on top of the quarterly Arbitron ratings. Usually, when one of those stations came in at No. 1, the other would be right behind at No. 2.

For years, the main morning drive guy at KRMG was a locally famous air personality—and a great one—named John Erling. And although we were competing, just as those overnight deejays across the country and I had competed, John and I were friends as well as competitors. We could talk to each other in a friendly way over the air and appear on each other's shows, both things I don't believe you could do in today's radio market. Sure, John and I were both trying as hard as we could to keep our stations on top, but that didn't mean we had to be enemies. Really, it was just the opposite.

Along with John and the overnight guys I've mentioned, I was fortunate to be friends with a lot of people who were on the air at the same time I was. I can't mention them all, but some of the deejays I'm still in touch with are Johnny Western, who was on KFDI in

Wichita; Arch Yancey down in Houston; and Dave Boyd, who had a great little real-country station in Vinita, Oklahoma called KITO.

I worked with so many great people at KVOO and before, folks I won't ever forget. I hate to be doing a list of 'em, because I know I'll leave out people who've been real important in my life. So I'd better apologize right now and hope whoever's left out can just chalk it up to old age and forgetfulness and know that I still love 'em.

I've talked some throughout the book about deejays and management people I remember well. Some of them are really radio legends around these parts, like Jack Fox, a guy I saw coming and going for the better part of 30 years. Jack was a super guy, very well-liked, with a tremendous following. He did mornings on KVOO at the same time I was doing *Billy Parker's Big Rigger Show*, and after I went to daytimes, my show came along right after his. He and Otto Dunn would come on at 5 a.m. every weekday, and we've had tons of great visits, both off the air and over the microphone.

Another talented nice guy I worked with real closely was Steve Jackson; he's in the nursing business now. One of the things I remember most about him is how good he was on the air. When I was operations director, I had some people working for me that I respected but maybe weren't quite as good at deejaying as I would've liked. I respected Steve a lot, and he was a fine disc jockey to boot.

Going back a ways, even before KVOO, there was Will Jones. He and his wife, Wilma, were just good people. I worked with him early in my career, around the same time I cut his "Gold Rush Girl" for the 4 Star label, which would have been back in '65.

THANKS—THANKS A LOT

Jack Campbell was at KVOO for many years, and he was one of the finest newsmen who ever walked. I admired what he did, how he could get right to the heart of a story and then, in a few sentences, tell it over the air so that anyone could understand it. We're friends to this day.

River Spirit Casino is one of the nicest and best-run gaming places in Oklahoma, and I know a lot of that has to do with Jerry Floyd, who's general manager there. Jerry also did some work for KVOO and me when he was a good old country-music deejay, one of the best we had. I'm glad to see that he's done so well for himself.

Jay Jones was a fine radio man, not only on the air as a news person, but as a *stature* person as well, if you know what I mean. He really had something to him. At one time, he pretty much *was* KVOO—the program director, a newsman, and a disc jockey, all at the same time.

Jim Jeffries, the old Hoot Owl, is *still* on a quest to keep real country music alive. We need a lot more like him in radio today: a really super guy who knows what he's doing on the air and genuinely respects the men and women who gave country music its foundation.

Just like there weren't a whole lot of Black artists in country music when I was in the business, there weren't a lot of Black men and women working at country radio either. One who did was my very good friend Richard Williams at KVOO. He worked mostly in the production end of things, and he was my go-to guy. He'd do anything in the world for you.

Because I was always involved in sales as well as the other parts of the business, I guess I tend to remember salesmen who were especially good at what they did. I'd put both Jim Munson and Ray Grime in that category. They were both at KVOO, and they were top-notch. So were Robin Carpenter and Jeannette Miller—super people, and still good friends of mine. Both of them were in sales at KVOO and Big Country 99.5. I worked with them a lot. They were very good with my clients and very good to me. And Robin is a great fisherman—or woman.

When I think back on those days, I sometimes think of the old song that Bob Wills's fiddler Jesse Ashlock wrote, "My Life's Been A Pleasure." Although I'm not saying there weren't some bumpy spots, it was a pleasure to do what I did, and it was the people around me who made it that way. I've talked about Opal Bledsoe at KVOO, who helped the Binghams and me pull the joke on Wooley during that *Wooley Wednesday* broadcast; we also had Shirley Speechley and Helen Riddell, receptionists at the studio and great people—good to me and good to KVOO. And there's not a finer person than Michelle Oatman, who came down from Wichita as Andy's assistant when Great Empire bought the station. Of course, she ended up marrying him, and those two people were very important in my life.

As I mentioned earlier, for the last 15 or so years I was broadcasting, Dennis McAtee was my right-hand man. As my engineer, he had the responsibility of making sure what went over the air matched what I had on my playlists, and he did it all while also dealing with the guests I'd have in the studio, who were sometimes so thick you couldn't stir 'em with a stick. He was always so good to everybody and never got rattled. (I wish I could say the same for myself.) I couldn't have had a show without him.

At the same time, we had Guy T. Miller out there in the wings. Guy wasn't with the station, but he was an avid record collector and big country-music fan who'd come through whenever we needed to find a certain song. I believe he has just about every CD and album you'd ever want, and he knows more about recorded music than just about anyone I can think of.

Then there are the artists. Over the years, I've been privileged to know, and work with, some of the greats. I've mentioned a lot of them already, but I want to make sure to get down in this book a couple more that I'm especially fond of, even if they may not have reached household-name status.

Peggy Rains, from Pryor, is just a wonderful singer and the nicest person you could imagine. I had the privilege of recording a couple of tunes with her, "I'll Never be Free" and "Ain't Nobody's Business But My Own," which were both first cut by Tennessee Ernie Ford and Kay Starr. Wooley, who plays our versions pretty regularly on his *Swing on This* show, swears that ours are better. I'm not too sure about that, but I'm sure that Peggy is one of the best people I've ever worked with.

If you know the name Jimmy Hall, you're probably a big western-swing fan. Jimmy was a vocalist, songwriter, and one of the fiddlers in Leon McAuliffe's Cimarron Boys, the band that "Take It Away, Leon" put together in Tulsa after World War II. I loved Jimmy and I loved his music, and it seems like we were always kind to one another. Like Peggy, Jimmy was one of those talented people who didn't get all the accolades they should've gotten.

As you know from other parts of this book, my being in radio—and with E.T.—put me in contact with pretty much all the biggest country-music artists of the day, including the ones whose music I loved the most. Those would be people like George Jones, Merle Haggard, and, I have to say, Ernest Tubb—artists who told it like it was, who put out songs that anyone could relate to. Cal Smith, too, who helped me so much in the business and was such a great entertainer. And Tammy Wynette. Like the rest of 'em, she told the kinds of stories you don't hear nowadays.

That's one of the big differences between then and now. Today, you don't hear the stories. You don't hear a lot of people like Red Steagall. I don't care if Red's singing about the Old West or doing one of his country songs—you can live it with him because you've lived it and you understand it. Along with Ernest, Cal Smith, and George Jones, Red is one of my favorite people.

I can say the same for Ray Price. He didn't do anything I didn't like—at least until he got to the point where he was using a big orchestra. I remember being in the Green Hornet with Ernest and the Troubadours and pulling up behind him in Shreveport, Louisiana, at that famous Municipal Memorial Auditorium where they did *The Louisiana Hayride* all those years. I think we were opening the show that night. We all parked, and about five of us got out of the Green Hornet. Ray had two or three buses, and people just *kept* coming out of 'em. There had to be at least 20 people in that great-big band he had.

I never had much acquaintance with people like George and Merle and Tammy until I started emceeing shows and got to know 'em a little. I don't want to make it sound like we were next-door neighbors. I don't want it to sound phony. But they liked me and I liked them.

At the same time, to be completely truthful with you, I never kidded myself about having any kind of big impact on their lives. We talked, I played their records and sometimes emceed their shows; they were in the scene and, in a lesser way, so was I.

Sometimes, though, they'd surprise you. I didn't really want to put this next story in the book, because it might make you feel like I think too highly of myself, that I believe I was some sort of big deal. But John and Brett talked me into it. They said it was a good story and ought to be told.

I've still got a qualm or two about it. But here it is, as told to Brett by Sunny Leigh, one of the best morning-drive deejays I've had the pleasure to know and work with.

"A few years ago," Sunny told Brett, "[the movie] *9 to 5* was made into a Broadway musical. Dolly Parton said, 'I'm going to do *one* interview for radio, so if you want your station to apply, here's the email address, and here's who to write, and I will pick one station.' So we applied, thinking there's no way she's going to choose us over all the other stations that would apply from around the nation.

"But, sure enough, she chose us.

"I went by Billy's desk to tell him. 'Hey,' I said, 'We've got Dolly Parton coming on. Didn't you work with her? Don't you know her?'

"He said, 'Oh, I *did*. But she wouldn't remember me.'

"I told him he was just being humble. 'Come on the interview and talk to her,' I said. 'You haven't talked to her in how long?' He said it had been years and years.

"'Well, come in the studio and we'll let you guys talk a little bit. We'll record it, and if it's good, we'll use it. It's history being made: Billy Parker and Dolly Parton.'

"He kind of pooh-poohed that, and he didn't come in [for the interview] the next morning. I was on the air at that time with Skip Mahaffey, and when she called we were all atwitter. We said, 'Hi—Dolly Parton hotline.'

"The first words out of her mouth were, 'This is Dolly. Where's Billy Parker?'

"Skip and I about died. We said, 'He thought you wouldn't remember him,' and she said, 'How could I forget Billy Parker?'

"We ran the interview, with her asking about Billy. Thinking back on it now, I'm sure she selected KVOO because of him."

BILLY PARKER'S "OVER AND OUT" | RETIREMENT PARTY | JANUARY 22ND, 2016 | CAIN'S BALLROOM

PHOTO COURTESY OF ROBIN CARPENTER SCHWERS

EPILOGUE

Even though I've been off the air for a few years now, I still get contacted from time to time by disc jockeys from around the country who are still playing my old records. Of course, I have to include Wooley on that list; he remembers to play a Parker song pretty regularly on his *Swing on This* public-radio show, which you can get on the radio or the computer at 7 p.m. Tulsa time every Saturday night. And I know there are several other deejays out there who are dedicated to keeping real country music alive, and those of us who love it should be grateful to them. One of the best is a guy named H.D. Ainsworth, who has *The Minden Morning Show* down in Louisiana, over radio station KBEF. I always enjoy visiting over the air with him, and I'm happy that he's playing some of my old songs.

When you put something out there, like a record or a book, you never really know what's going to happen. *I* don't, anyway. In fact, around the time I was leaving radio. I was surprised when I got a message from a fellow down around Nashville named Charlie Ammerman, who'd been in the business a long time and worked with a lot of big names. He had a label called Pretty World Records, and he wanted to know if he could release some of my old songs. I said sure, and before I knew it, I was getting reports from a publication called *IndieWorld*, which had a chart for independent country-music records.

I'm proud to say that on August 19, 2016, the recording of mine that has become my signature song over the years, the track that's been on more of my albums than any other, the one I'll forever associate with Jerri, hit the very top of those charts. Finally, with "Lord, If I Make It to Heaven," Billy Parker had his first No. 1 single.

And honestly, folks, I can't think of a better ending for this book.

JOHN WOOLEY

JOHN WOOLEY has written, co-written, or edited nearly 50 books, including his previous collaboration with Brett Bingham, *Twentieth-Century Honky-Tonk*, the story of Tulsa's legendary Cain's Ballroom. He also spent several years working with his friend Billy Parker on KVOO's *Wooley Wednesday* western-swing program. His most recent works include the critically acclaimed Cleansing horror trilogy (*Seventh Sense, Satan's Swine,* and *Sinister Serpent*), all written with Robert A. Brown, and *Right Down the Middle*, the as-told-to biography of the New York Yankees pitching great Ralph Terry. A four-time finalist for the Oklahoma Book Award, Wooley was the first writer ever to be inducted into the Oklahoma Music Hall of Fame.

BRETT BINGHAM

BRETT BINGHAM broke into print in 2020 with *Twentieth-Century Honky-Tonk*, an experience positive enough to lead to this second collaboration with his co-writer, John Wooley. Like Wooley, he and Billy Parker have been friends for many years. In fact, Brett's music-business work with his uncle, the legendary producer and booking agent Ray Bingham, has led to many enduring friendships and opportunities. Brett is also the business manager for Bob Wills' Texas Playboys under the direction of Jason Roberts, the newest incarnation of the famed western-swing band—all of this in addition to his corporate world day-job. Preserving musical history is one of the most important things in Brett's life, as are his daughters, Jessica and Tori.

INDEX

A
Air Force, 13–14
Artco, 142–43
Autry, Gene, 5, 7, 15, 98, 140, 212

B
Beanee Weenees, 88–89
Big Country Music Guide, 117, 146
Big Rigger Club, 105
Big Rigger Show, 106, 109, 115, 133, 137, 151, 153, 159
Billboard, 7, 114, 143, 146, 161
Bill Haynes Company, 135, 190–91
Billy Parker Golf Classic, 196, 198–99
Bingham, Brett, 239, 245
Bingham, Ray, 39, 65, 147, 180, 185, 239
Black artists in country music, 250
Blue, Ron, 33–34, 62, 206

Bradley, Owen, 67–68, 82, 93, 141
Bryant, Donald, 14
Byrd, Tracy, 215, 217–18

C
Cain's Ballroom, 7, 11, 21, 46, 55, 68–69, 79, 216, 224
Cale, Johnny, 43
Canada, 220
Chapel, Jean, 59
Chapman, Steve, 76, 88, 95–96
Charleton, Buddy, 76, 88, 95–96
Christmas songs, 167–68
church, 4, 221–22
Coleman, James, 25
Colorado, 27, 30–33
Country Junction, 219, 236, 238–39
Country Music Association, 145, 153

Country Music Award, 155
Country Music Disc Jockey Hall of Fame, 229
Country Music Hall of Fame, 230
Cresse, Jack, 98, 100, 102, 117, 154–55, 189

D

DeMarco, Mike, 210, 230–31, 234
Disc Jockey Hall of Fame, 230–31
DJ Convention, 153–54
Dutsch, Dennis, 110–11
Duvall, Bob, 22–23

E

education of Billy Parker, 16, 20, 31
Emery, Ralph, 99
Ernest Tubb Record Shop, 75, 77
E-Z Chord, 195–96

F

Foley, Red, 24–25, 30, 84

G

Gibson, Betty, 175–76
God, 221–22
Grand Ole Opry, 3, 6, 13–14, 63, 75, 80, 153

Great Empire, 210, 233–34, 251
Greene, Jack, 68, 70, 78, 94, 114
Green Hornet, 77–78, 83, 88, 253
Guthrie, Jack, 225

H

Halsey, Jim, 104, 113, 117–18
Hartman, Tom, 143
Hee Haw, 112, 183–84
Hitchcock, Stan, 29, 36, 185
house bands, 32, 133, 193, 223
Hunt, John, 205–6

I

independent labels, 173–74
Ingles, David, 37, 39, 41, 45, 51, 54, 140
International Country Gospel Music Association, 222

J

Jernigan, Wayne, 76, 95–96
Jolly Green Giants, 70, 82
Jones, Fred, 37–38, 209
Jones
   George, 39, 253
   Haze, 94, 102
Journal Broadcast Group, 233–34, 236, 238

K

KVOO, 37, 98–101, 104, 167, 205–7, 213, 237

L

Lang, Cyrina, 199–200
Latting, Bob, 22–23
Lee, Brenda, 24–25, 57, 173
Lee, Johnnie, 8, 21, 46, 49, 66, 176–77, 224
Lewis, Bobby, 78, 85
Longhorn Wingding, 61–62
Lynch, Mike, 63, 167, 209, 233
Lynn, Loretta, 93, 107–8

M

Mack, Bill, 99–100, 104, 152–53, 189, 248
Marijohn, 23–25, 29
Maxey, Austin, 42–43, 124
Mayo, O.W., 7–8, 66, 69, 215, 226
McAtee, Dennis, 234, 241, 251
McCall, Darrell, 175–76, 178, 226
McCullough, Marvin, 49, 51
McCurdy, Pat, 144
McDaniel, Mel, 44–45
McEntire, Pake, 150
Midnite Jamboree, 75–76, 80
Miller, Ernie, 192–93
Moore, Joe, 191–92

O

Oatman, Mike, 167, 209, 233–34
Oklahoma Guide, 42–43
Oklahoma Music Hall of Fame, 239–40
Overstreet, Tommy, 114–15, 147, 170
Ozark Jubilee, 24–25

P

Parton, Dolly, 82, 183, 245
Party Barn, 110
Paxton, Gary, 141–43
payola, 163–64
Pierce, Webb, 24, 177–78
Poovey, Joe, 59
Porter Wagoner Show, 183
Powell, Buddy, 103–4
Pride Records, 41–43, 138

Q

QuikTrip, 32–33, 110

R

Rogues Five, 43–44
Ruff, Ray, 174

S

Seely, Jeannie, 73, 78, 82, 138, 238
Silver Dollar Band, 180–82

Sims Records, 58–59, 226, 229
Smith, Cal, 55, 67, 70, 76, 94, 178, 253
Soundwaves, 175
Stanley, Noel, 95–96
Steagall, Red, 217, 239, 246, 253
Stonehorse, 179–80, 246
Stuart, Harold, 98, 101, 204, 209, 211–12
Sunshine Country, 144–45, 147–48, 172–73, 222
Sunshine Country Records, 109, 138, 144–45

T
Talbert, Brenda, 180
Tener Records, 43
Texas, 133, 147, 192
Texas Playboys, 98, 147, 198, 223
Texas Troubadours, 68, 71, 75, 80–81, 93, 224
Thayer, David, 180–81
Thompson, Hank, 198, 230–31, 239
Tramel, Jimmie, 245–46
Trimm, Bobby Dee, 144
truck drivers, 104–6, 136
Tubb, Ernest, 55, 73, 79, 83–86, 226, 244
Tulsa Camera Record and Triangle Blueprint, 20
Tulsa Playboys, 47, 246
Tulsa Roughnecks, 198
Tulsa Stampede, 66
Tulsa Theater, 6

Tulsa World, 236, 245
Turner, Grant, 63–64, 77

U
Uptown Club, 55–56

W
Western, Johnny, 34, 212, 248
Williams, Hank, 6, 84, 238
Wills
    Bob, 8, 46, 83, 214
    Johnnie Lee, 8, 11, 21, 49, 66, 145, 176–77, 214
Wisconsin, 77–78
women, 108, 110, 250
Wooley, John, 196, 212, 245
Wooley Wednesday, 213–14, 219, 225

Y
YouTube, 181–82, 184

ACKNOWLEDGEMENTS

Billy, Brett, and John extend special thanks to Stephanie, Dave, and Gloria Pierce of Dave's Claremore RV; Dr. Joe Moore of Moore Funeral Homes and Cremation Service; Michelle Oatman; and Jeannette Miller. Their kind generosity helped make *Thanks— Thanks A Lot* a reality.

Thanks also to the talented folks at Mullerhaus Legacy, who were instrumental in crafting this book: Kristin Stroup, Alexandra Seifried, Jared Casci, Laura Hyde, Kayloni Alexander, and Doug Miller. And, of course, to William Bernhardt and the whole Bernhardt family at Babylon Books, our publisher.

www.ingramcontent.com/pod-product-compliance
Lightning Source LLC
Chambersburg PA
CBHW011405070526
44577CB00003B/385